JOHN W. VANNORSDALL

Reflections
on the Gospel
After a Time Away

Dimly
Burning
Wicks

FORTRESS PRESS   Philadelphia

Library of Congress Cataloging in Publication Data

Vannorsdall, John W.
Dimly burning wicks.

1. Meditations.   I. Title.
BV4832.2.V373   242'.5   81-70661
ISBN 0-8006-1622-7   AACR2

9393L81   Printed in the United States of America   1-1622

In Memory Of

Edith Overmyer Vannorsdall
1900–1980

William Warren Vannorsdall
1899–1965

Contents

Foreword

There are a variety of ways of understanding the gospel of Jesus Christ, and that distresses some people, though I am not among them. When I was a child, I heard and saw a simple version of the gospel which served me well. As my life and questions became more complex, I was introduced to understandings of the gospel profound enough and more, to keep pace with my growing need.

I was fortunate. Others in large numbers have distanced themselves from the church because the simpler version of the gospel no longer embraces the long reach of their minds and hearts. They are embarrassed by spiritual coats with sleeves too short and pants which look like knickers.

The pages which follow are responsive to only a few of the questions we have learned to ask. They assume only that one person's search might be helpful to others. The first nine chapters center on God's disclosure of himself, with Christmas and Easter as focal points. The remaining six chapters center on ways of responding to the claim which God makes. Each chapter is discrete and yet integral to what is explored in all of the others.

Many of the images in these pages were created for sermons first given in Battell Chapel at Yale University, for the Protestant Radio Hour, or for convocations in other parts of the country. To all who have helped to evoke and sharpen these understandings, and particularly the people who worship at Battell, I am deeply indebted.

JOHN VANNORSDALL

Behold my servant, whom I uphold,
   my chosen, in whom my soul delights;
I have put my Spirit upon him,
   he will bring forth justice to the nations.
He will not cry or lift up his voice,
   or make it heard in the street;
a bruised reed he will not break,
   and a dimly burning wick he will not quench;
   he will faithfully bring forth justice.
He will not fail or be discouraged
   till he has established justice in the earth;
   and the coastlands wait for his law.

Isaiah 42:1–4

1 | A Dimly Burning Wick

Some people are twice born Christians. They were born of natural parents, and born again of the Holy Spirit. I rejoice with them. They have found refreshment in their experience of God. There are others of us, however, who are not twice born, but twice burned. The chapters which follow have been written with the twice burned in mind. These are the people, and I have been among them, who have been touched by the church and the gospel at one or more times in their lives but instead of being healed, have been hurt by that experience. Nevertheless, for many of us, there are still embers of faith, a few glowing coals in the hearth of our souls. My intention is to blow lightly on these embers in hope that faith may come alive.

I do this, of course, out of my own need, but also because I perceive the wistfulness with which many of the twice burned behold the embers of their religious experience. Like people who have been on a long journey, we sit now at the end of the evening before the fireplace and wonder where this journey has taken us and where hope and meaning are to be found for the journey yet to come.

Part of this late evening contemplation is the remembrance of what the church, God, and Christ have really meant to us. Some of it was important, you see, or there would be no embers at all. Each of us has his or her own story. For some it is the still lingering image of a parent, hands folded in prayer, or the sound of the organ and the singing of hymns. Others of us can still see the colors dancing on the sill of the stained glass window as the tree in the churchyard swayed gently in the summer morning breeze. There is the still lingering image of the candlelit

church on Christmas Eve, and "Silent Night" sung with hidden
tears, the cadenced rhythm of the catechism, the incense of a
building closed for most of the week, Sunday school basement
and lakeside summer camp.

What did it all mean? What does it mean to us now that years
ago, at Thanksgiving and other times, we held hands around
the table and offered prayer to the unseen God present within
the circle of our arms? It meant that we had some larger
framework within which to understand ourselves, however dim
its outline. We had a beginning, and his name was God. It was
God who stood beside us when we were sick and when trouble
came. God's people were our longer history. He brought us out
of Egypt and gave us laws for knowing what was good and
what must be avoided. He came among us in human form so
that we could better see and hear him. Christ suffered for our
sins, and we had some feel for what sin was. He was raised
again so that we could have a sign that our sins do not put an
end to God's love.

Something happened to this framework of meaning, this
elaborate tapestry of faith, this firelight of our early trusting.

One part of what happened was our neglect. We started doing other things in high school, or when we went to college. We
established distance from our parents and from our parents'
religion. We saw the minister or priest less often, heard the
organ and saw the dancing colors less often, seldom sang the
hymns or heard the rhythm of the scriptures. Our faith was not
fed, until only the embers remained. It was like a trumpet no
longer played, long left on the closet shelf; something from
childhood past and no longer done.

But what also happened was that we encountered people who
did not believe in God, in prayers or hymns, that Christ had
come, or that there was any transcendent vision to be had, any
source beyond a cosmic accident, or any end beyond the grave.
And since we had stopped growing in our understanding of our
faith, we hardly had an answer for ourselves, let alone an
answer for the doubts that others raised within us.

It was more than that, however. We had begun to worship

other gods. Good health, good looks, and good grades. Sex was a more important vision, success a more insistent law. Moreover, we had been burned by the church. Some of us the church simply forgot, perhaps because we went away. Others of us were forgotten in another sense. The church forgot that we were older now and our questions more probing, and the church did not invite or help us to go deeper into its treasure of insight and understanding. Some of us were burned because we believed so simply that God's people were like Christ, and then discovered in our new and larger place just how limited the church's impact was upon a world of poverty, prejudice, and privilege. We discovered the distance between Christ and his people.

Some of us were burned by the prohibitions of the church, by the too simple explanations of what was right. We heard so many negative things about sex that even when married we found it difficult to enter with assurance into the pleasures of the marital relationship. We heard so much about the presence of God that we were unprepared for the long absences of God. We heard so much about turning to God for answers to our prayers that we found it hard to affirm the legitimacy of the intellectual enterprise, the right to make our own decisions and to accept the consequences.

So now, with longing, we sit before the hearth of our spirits and contemplate the embers of our faith. We've matured enough to know that other gods have not served us well. We know that our pursuit of power and accomplishment leaves us always hungry. We have enough experience in the world to know that in the cause of social justice the church and her people at least honor the goal, while much of the world has become cynical and cares not at all.

It's in the midst of late night reflection on these things that the words of Isaiah have their meaning for me, and perhaps for you: "He will not cry or lift up his voice, or make it heard in the street; a bruised reed he will not break, and a dimly burning wick he will not quench; he will faithfully bring forth justice in the earth, and the coastlands wait for his law." There are so many of us who are bruised reeds and dimly burning wicks, wearied into a laid-back time in our living. If we remember former times when faith in God was strong and wonder if it is possible to return, then it is important to know that a dimly burning wick he will not quench.

Not that we can return to what we once experienced in Christianity, or that we want to do so. But perhaps we are prepared to find new and deeper things in the half-remembered story. Not just that God draws near, but also the witness that God is often absent, even for those men and women of the largest faith, and that this is no more threatening or unexpected than the lulls in the fever of a marriage or a friendship.

Many of us were taught, when we were young, that material things — especially our bodies — were the root of all evil. It was gospel truth that all sexual attraction was rooted in lust, that a cadaverous countenance was the mark of holiness, and that nice people didn't talk about money. We've matured now, enough to hear the whole gospel, which names the worst of our sins as sins of the spirit and teaches that material things, including our sexuality, are gifts of God.

Since we are more perceptive about the power of sin to undercut our own best intentions to behave justly, it should be possible for us to enter into the church's struggle for justice with far less cynicism. And since we ourselves are broken reeds, we may be prepared to hear with fresh desire the witness of the gospel that freedom comes by the grace of God and not by our perfection; that even broken reeds have their work in the kingdom which is both now and coming.

Some things will never be the same. While we've been gone, they've changed the hymns, the liturgies and prayers, and many of the people we used to know will not be there, their places taken by others like ourselves returning after long absence. Nevertheless, as you will recognize in the pages which follow, it is the same ancient story of the Creator who beheld his creation gone wrong, who came one Christmas Eve to be among us. It is still the story of love acting to heal, of love come to death, and of hope restored. Above all, it is a story about freedom for new beginnings. And if our need or desire is strong enough and we take up where we once left off, Isaiah's words will be proven true: "a bruised reed he will not break and a dimly burning wick he will not quench."

I wait for the Lord, my soul waits,
  and in his word I hope;
my soul waits for the Lord
  more than watchmen for the morning,
  more than watchmen for the morning.
O Israel, hope in the Lord!
  For with the Lord there is steadfast love,
  and with him is plenteous redemption.

Psalm 130:5-7

2 | Waiting

There was a time when waiting meant that we weren't old enough for something. Since we were confident of our immediate readiness, waiting had no redeeming qualities at all. In fact, the "go-go" temper of American culture turned waiting into a downright bad thing to do. It was no different in our churches. The imperative laid upon us was that we "decide for Christ," and that the time for doing that was right now, before we left this service or at least before this particular "crusade" was over. What could it possibly mean to "wait for the Lord," and what good could come of it?

What the years have taught is not only that waiting is a normal part of the human experience, but that waiting is the arms of welcome half-circled to receive that which has not yet come; arms which describe the shape of that which we desire to receive.

When it comes to the experience of God, an expectant openness to the possibility of his coming is the most important thing we have to contribute. But waiting for the Lord is different from other kinds of waiting.

Most of our waiting is the ordinary kind. I put the coffee water on the stove in the morning and wait for it to boil—but not really, because I drink my juice, let the cat come in or out, pour the cereal in a bowl, and by then the water's ready and I haven't thought much of anything at all. Waiting for a taxi is something different because I hate to call until I'm ready in case it comes right away, which it never does; so waiting is hard, and I pace back and forth afraid that I will miss my train. But what does it mean to wait for the Lord?

Somehow it's not like ordinary waiting. Not like waiting for the water to boil or the first day of school. It's not like waiting for the prayer to end, the hymn to begin, the telephone to ring. Not like waiting for day's end when we can turn back the covers and turn out the light.

It's more like waiting for a certain woman or a certain man. We'd seen this other before, walking, talking with friends, so self-assured and yet with something saved, held back, some inner life reserved for another time. But it seemed as though this one who stood out among all the others was well beyond our possibility, as though he or she belonged in another class, with another group of people each more attractive than ourselves, some quality which put us in his or her shadow. And then one day she came, he came, to talk with us, or maybe only smiled, but something inside of us knew that we had been acknowledged, invited to share a private word or longing which would be ours alone, something between the two of us. And with great care, with the rhythm and grace of ballet, we drew near and moved away. We ate together, prepared a meal together, were silent together and shared our stories of times gone by, our good times and the things which made us afraid. And soon our world revolved around this other. We knew the other's walk and each movement of the face and tone of voice, and our lives were somehow re-created in this person. This was the one for whom we waited with such longing, such expectation. And our waiting for the Lord is more like waiting for a man or a woman than like waiting for the water to boil or for the first day of school. It's like waiting for a man or a woman; except that waiting for the Lord is not that private or that exclusive.

"My soul waits for the Lord more than watchmen for the morning, more than watchmen for the morning." I wait for something large enough to reshape the whole of my life — something large enough to gather me up, and all those around me; to turn us in a common direction and make us friends. I wait for all the lights to go out, for the whole city to lose its electricity, for a time when I am drawn into the hallway with my candle and my neighbors with theirs, where in the soft light they say to me, "I wonder what happened. The whole city is out." And I say, "I wonder how long it will be." And together we go in search of the elevator to see if anyone is stuck in it and needing help. When we come back, I say, "I was just about to have some soup. Won't you come and join me while it is still hot?" And they come, which had never happened before the lights went out: that I and my neighbors were together sharing food and conversation. It's not like ordinary waiting, this waiting for the Lord. It's like waiting for his act by which he transforms the ordinary, an act which creates the possibility of something new — an act of God which unleashes the laws which bind, and brings forth looting; but also neighbors sitting down to soup and glad that something has happened large enough to be a bridge twelve feet long from door to door.

Waiting for the Lord is like waiting for some astonishing news to greet us in the morning — that a snowstorm has closed all the offices, schools, and stores, and we come alive with new possibilities of things to be done with the day. We shovel to our neighbors' door in hope that there'll be some need of us and that the neighbors will be glad we came. It's like waiting for a snowstorm which transforms an ordinary day into a day that's radically different.

It's like waiting for a war, this waiting for the Lord. Perverse, but true for those of us able to remember some of the feelings of World War II, and how that also gathered us and shook the gloom of the Depression, changed the tune, and called us to concern for one another's sons and daughters; how we talked to people we'd never met, with deep compassion sometimes. It was a time when we did extraordinary things, took bizarre trips, and told incredible stories; and suffered incredibly, too. It was the worst and the best of times. Like waiting for that kind of wartime, we wait for the Lord.

In some ways waiting for Christmas is like waiting for the Lord. Christmas has all the power of a blackout, a snowstorm, or war. To set up a tree in the house, to bake special cookies, take time from work, set aside money, to gather in whomever we can of friends and family, to surround ourselves with special music of great power; these things together create a radical change in what is ordinary in our lives. It is a magic time in which old wounds can be healed, forgiveness be offered and accepted, a time for love and for reaching out. Christmas is a time for lovers, a private time, but it is larger than one person or even two. Christmas embraces our whole world, the largest of our hopes and dreams, not just for ourselves but for all people. In fact, we know that it would not be Christmas for one or for lovers if it did not evoke some larger setting in which all of us become, for a brief but glorious time, a part of the extended family of God. To wait for Christmas is something like what it means to wait for the Lord.

All of the elements are known to us. Everything that it means to wait for the Lord. And yet it is the Lord for whom my soul waits, and not the first day of school, the lover, or Christmas. They are like rain running down the window screen, filling each tiny square of my life with water, but the drop moves on, and behind it the squares wink, and the water is gone. The lights of the city will come on again, and I must blow out my candle and my neighbors theirs as they cross the blackout bridge from my door to theirs, and I must go back to yesterday's living.

And what shall we say of the man or the woman who re-created our lives? It may be that they are already gone, and our lives changed again, this time by grief or sadness. Or, if still living with this other in warm pleasure, then we discover that this relationship, which at its start was so dramatic and longed for, is now simply the center of the web of ordinary things, and constant reminder that what is central for a time is always subject to death, and our life with another is no surety against darkness.

Christmas itself is so time bound that even as the day begins we are aware of its ending, and that short days from now we'll be back at work, the tree will come down and we must yet face the coldest days of winter.

It is for the Lord of Christmas that my soul waits.

I wait for the Lord who was before I began to be, who knows the world from its beginning, and is not afraid of its great size and empty places. The Lord who, for whatever reason, I cannot guess, will not stay away embarrassed by a peopled sphere which went always wrong from its beginning, but who draws near to wait with those who wait for him. I wait for the Lord who is angry and filled with indignation when people shoot one another, cheat one another, and spill oil on white sand beaches. I wait for the Lord who in a great parabola of grace enters the atmophere of time and space, is bound to a cross by the weight of human sin, and swoops on down into the hell of all time's making; the Lord, who arching up again through Easter's tomb, brings with him all who wait for him and desire to live in the light and to sing the songs of freedom.

I wait for the Lord who doesn't boil and cool again, like the coffee water on the stove. I wait for the Lord whose love is lasting, who stirs me for longer than a one-night blackout, a snowstorm which reorders just a single day. I wait for the Lord who challenges me to find in the love of another human being both a model and a strength for giving my life to a larger world of always particular people who live in shadows waiting for me. I wait for the Lord whose Christmas lights are always burning, who sends a band of angels singing, each day a pillar of cloud and each night a fire to lead us out of every time of bondage. I wait for his promised time when we shall beat our swords into plowshares and our spears into pruning hooks; when nation shall not lift up sword against nation.

We may wait a long time, but we know for whom we wait. And our waiting is the most important thing we have to contribute. It is the half-circled arms of our waiting which describe him for whom we wait, as our waiting itself begins to give shape to what we desire to become.

"I wait for the Lord, my soul waits, and in his word I hope."

For every boot of the tramping warrior in battle
    tumult
  and every garment rolled in blood
  will be burned as fuel for the fire.
For to us a child is born,
  to us a son is given;
and the government will be upon his shoulder,
  and his name will be called
  "Wonderful Counselor, Mighty God,
  Everlasting Father, Prince of Peace."

Isaiah 9:5–6

3 | *To Us A Child Is Given*

The woods are neither cool nor dark, but splotchy. The white pines still have most of their needles, but the oak and white and yellow birch are bare as autumn, and in between, the tips of maple branches show their perforations. Gypsy moths are voracious. I fight the Gypsy moths, but I understand their right to behave as they do.

Last year I spent days cutting and pulling down the wild grape vines which had climbed to the tops of the tallest trees, and now, their strength renewed by spring rains, they've begun to climb again. The porcupines, by a constant eating of the leaves, have killed the young birch behind the house and now have bitten down the blackberries. In our garden of New England soil, the winter's freeze and thawing have pushed up boulders so large we must use a block and tackle to remove them.

I have no complaint about any of this. I save what I can and fight back to make a space for things I'd like to grow, to keep the water flowing in the stream, the rain from entering the house.

I have less patience with the depredations of human beings, with the aggressiveness and violence which we practice against one another. It's not just the shootings of presidents and popes, the slaying of an archbishop or the blood on the floor of underground prisons in a dozen countries around the world. What disturbs me more is that these gross abuses of one another are the outcroppings of a more pervasive violence which occurs in almost every home, supermarket, office, and school. I could be righteously indignant about it except for the violence I experience within myself, not far beneath the surface of my decently ordered life.

I have no doubt that we, too, are a part of nature, responding to some ancient instinct for self-preservation. I know that we are more than that. At least we can imagine life without violence, and I know that I have some capacity to control my anger and to alter the patterns of cool calculation by which I demean other people. That's the least of it. I also have the capacity to enhance the lives of others, to provide them space and nurture for their own sense of worth and dignity.

What I am not able to control is the violence which is directed against me. None of us, living in contemporary America, is completely safe from at least potential abuse at the hands of others. This seems to be particularly true for those of us who live in cities. My experience, five break-ins in six years, may not be typical, but I meet too many people who have experienced robbery or assault to believe that my experience is worse than that of many others. What concerns me, as one who abhors violence, is that I reply upon fully armed men and women, the police, to protect me. In a world as violent as ours, even the not violent depend upon legalized violence to curb the violence we deplore. I see no way out of this dilemma.

To admit that I am dependent upon legalized violence for my protection, however, does not mean that there is nothing more to be said. It demeans aggressors to excuse their actions because they were themselves abused, or were victims themselves. These excuses in their behalf rob them of their dignity as decision markers and therefore people to be held accountable. Nevertheless, it is true that we have built an economic system without a place for everyone. We have set criteria for being successful which not everyone can achieve. We have tolerated violence toward women and children. Our myths of heroism are the myths of frontier violence and warfare. Though I prefer a world in which I need not be protected from violence by violence, I cannot do that. What I can do is to accept my complicity in the evocation of the violence I encounter, and to speak and vote for a society which produces fewer violent people. I choose to be protected by the police, but I am committed to the creation of a society in which fewer police are neccessary and are called upon less often.

I am also uncomfortable with the violence which marks the biblical story. I'm no more comfortable with Egyptian soldiers being drowned in the sea than I am with the execution of political dissidents. The Canaanites slain by the Jews as they entered the land were no less victims than the Cambodians slain by American bombs, Vietnamese rifles, and at the hands of their own countrymen in the name of communism. One could make the case that biblical violence is always on the side of justice, always visited upon the hosts of darkness by or in the name of God. I prefer not to travel that road. Too many people have died as the result of holy causes.

I prefer to emphasize the other biblical witness, and thereby admit a bias. Having been burned too often by the lifted sword of righteousness and seen it fall too often on the heads of others, I am drawn now to Isaiah's suffering servant, the one who had done no violence and yet would have divided to him a portion with the great. I am drawn to Christmas and the mangered child. Some will say that I must take the whole Bible and make it sing a single song. I weary of the intellectual gymnastics necessary to accomplish that and prefer to respond to what I perceive to be God's fullest disclosure of himself: his coming as a child.

The meaning of Christmas is, in many ways, no different for me than for most people. It is the remembrance of love and peace and shared hopes over many years, gathered now into one great longing. But in addition to that, which I would neither deny nor want to deny, I am now drawn to the quietness and nonaggressiveness of the Christmas event, to the absence of violence.

So much of the Christmas story suggests quietness. We assume that it was evening when the family arrived in Bethlehem, the noise of the streets hushed, the door of the shed closed, soft straw, softness of lamplight, the undisturbing sounds of the animals welcoming night, accepting the visitors who had come to join them. "How silently, how silently, the wondrous gift is given." Birth cry, no doubt, but it's not long before the child, too, is sleeping.

I'm not very sentimental about babies, but I am in awe of their vulnerability. It's easy to receive and cradle a baby. There is some anxiety because we know that we can hurt them, but we know that a baby cannot hurt us.

And one of the meanings of Christmas is that God doesn't want to hurt me or you. He desires that we receive him and not be afraid. There was a time when it would never have occurred to me to be afraid of God. But the more I've seen of myself and of the world, the better I've understood that we might be afraid of God.

One night there was an accident on the city street where I live most of the year and, without provocation, one driver began to beat the other who seemed shy and retiring. I was angry and came closer than I had in decades to striking another person. What must happen within God when he sees the way in which we beat one another? Consider all the battered children and beaten wives. One commentator estimates that women or children are beaten badly in at least one out of two American homes. What must it be like for God to watch our cruelty, the digging of graves to receive those dead at our hands long before their time?

The more I understand this, the more I know that we might well be afraid of God, and the more remarkable that he comes as a child.

We may not actually strike people, but we participate in violence in other ways. Most of us are well off in terms of having enough food, clothing, and adequate shelter. More important, we have processes of government which protect our freedom of speech, the sanctity of our homes, the freedom to acquire wealth, and a large measure of equality before the law. Most of us would not readily give up either what we possess as material things or our legal rights. In fact, most of us would fight to keep what we have — for oil if our own wells run dry or if other countries deny us the oil which they possess. And that's the meaning of the missiles nestled in our fields and cradled in our submarines. That's the meaning of our increased production of armaments and the funds spent for chemical and bacteriological warfare. We are all a part of this, not willingly perhaps, but we are not thereby excused. So God must watch his whales die and our submarines increase. It's not strange at all that we should fear the wrath of an angry God.

And that's what makes it so remarkable that when God comes to address his self-disclosing Word to us, that Word becomes a child. A child announced by singing, not by thunder. A child born by lamplight in the late night silence, rather than a Word which shakes the mountains. The Word of God comes to us as a child who can be received and cannot hurt us; a Word which does not make us afraid. I am prepared for the anger of God and believe that he has a right to wrath. What is amazing is that when he comes among us, whatever his righteous indignation, he comes not in violence, but defenseless against our further hurt, that we may receive rather than fear him.

I understand why some people become grim when the virginity of Mary is questioned and when the Revised Standard Version of the Bible translates Isaiah to read, "a young woman." Somehow they conceive of the Bible as a house of cards which, when one is removed, the whole of it collapses. I find the Bible to be made of sturdier stuff; made of the posts and beams of human joy and anguish over centuries, pinned with the pegs of insight, and bearing within it the yearning of God to disclose himself. What is disclosed in the Christmas story has nothing to do with whether or not Mary was a virgin. That claim is nothing more, nor less, than the praise of a people who believed that what happened in Bethlehem was of God's doing. They said that it was of God by saying that Mary was a virgin. Some have reversed it by saying that because Mary was a virgin, the event must be of God.

Those of us who have come some distance from the church of our early years cannot return by way of the bridge of proofs and houses of cards. But those of us who live in a world of violence might well be drawn to what is central in the Christmas story: the peaceful and vulnerable advent of Almighty God.

The contrasts between our life and God's coming are striking.

We are so often victims in the hands of the powerful. The professors tell us by wisecrack or sneer that they know the truth, and we are ignorant. Nurses tell us that this medication is good for us, but withhold its name and purpose. A waiter in a restaurant, often himself abused, is skilled at retaliation and incisive in naming our properly unimportant place in his scheme of things. A clerk in a government office ignores us, shuffles papers, and names our private affairs in a loud voice, committing an act of violence against us. A book salesman, a Bible salesman, just come from a psych-up session, will not hear our quiet no, but continues to push and tease.

In such ways distance is created. How can I receive others when by experience I know that I will be abused? And how can I give myself to others when there is so much anger and defensiveness within myself?

The violence of a sonic boom which shakes the house, the violence of a belching smokestack which leaves a dark film upon the windows — these things evoke anger within me. There is the violence of buildings without windows, too many people in too few rooms, radios too loud, a bottle rolling down a tenement stair, in every joke made about another race, in every refusal to yield to a passerby, every angry blare of the horn and splash of muddy water. There is violence in our sullen withdrawal from those to whom we are most closely bound.

In the midst of all of this which is our daily life and anguish, a story is told, the witness of the Christian community is made, about the way in which the Holy One makes himself known. "For to us a child is born, to us a son is given; . . . and his name will be called . . . Prince of Peace." However deep the hurt of God, whatever the anger which rises within him at each of our abuses of one another, he comes among us vulnerable, evoking awe but not fear, inviting our presence but not commanding it. There are neither drums nor cannon, but a band of angels singing, lamplight, and silence.

Those of us who live in the midst of violence, who dread it within ourselves and the distance which it creates between ourselves and others — many of us care little whether Mary was a virgin. There is another and overwhelming aspect of the Christmas story which draws us to Bethlehem. It is the lack of threat and violence there, the quiet vulnerability which allows us to come without fear. There is the hope that drawn close to such a God, the violence of our own lives might be stilled, and the peacefulness of his coming find place for growth within us.

"From the days of John the Baptist until now the kingdom of heaven has suffered violence, and men of violence take it by force . . . . But to what shall I compare this generation? It is like children sitting in the market places and calling to their playmates, 'We piped to you, and you did not dance; we wailed, and you did not mourn.' "

Matthew 11:12, 16–17

4 | *The Violent Bear It Away*

At our rural summer home, they come close to noon on a Sunday morning. As we sit at the kitchen table drinking coffee and reading the *New York Times*, the dog barks, and at the bottom of the drive two neatly dressed people get out of their car and head up toward the house.

We know, even before we notice the Bible, that we are about to be visited by a team of evangelists. The sinking feeling is in part because what's coming is so predictable. When other people walk up the drive, we go to the door with curiosity or expectation. One day it was a lady who had run off the road, and another day it was a man whose golden retriever had run away. More often someone is lost, and helping them find the right road is satisfying. But a team of evangelists?

Frustration and confusion combine to evoke just a touch of anger. It's frustrating because you know from previous experience that a true conversation will not be possible. They have come to tell you something, to share a commitment which they have made, and while they will be patient to hear your views, they are really not interested in them — only waiting until you finish so that they can get on with their mission of telling you the truth as they see it. Even if you tell them from the outset that you are a Christian, they will continue their testimony, convinced before they started toward your door that you don't possess the true way of understanding the gospel.

There is some inner confusion, too. If people have been granted an insight which creates joy and purpose in life, they should share it. They come with a gift, a personal and important gift. I understand that. I'm confused because what my head understands, my emotions reject.

29

There is also a sense of guilt in our reaction. The clarity and conviction of the evangelists remind us that we, too, were once secure in our faith, and they make us feel like failures for having fallen from certainty. Our minds tell us that we are still Christians, and with a more profound understanding of the gospel than was possible at an earlier time. But they make us defensive, as though we had run like cowards from the field of battle.

There is also a sense of violation. Our homes may not be castles, but they are, however grand or humble, a sacred space. It we want to drink coffee and read the *Times*, that's our privilege, and we'd like to do it uninterrupted, thank you! But since we welcome other strangers at the door, there must be more to it. They aren't just visitors. They come to tell us what to believe and how to live, and there is a violence in that against which we'd prefer to close and lock the door.

Flannery O'Connor took the title of her novel *The Violent Bear It Away* from the Gospel of Matthew. "From the days of John the Baptist until now the kingdom of heaven has suffered violence, and men of violence take it by force. . . . But to what," said Jesus, "shall I compare this generation? It is like children sitting in the market places and calling to their playmates, 'We piped to you, and you did not dance; we wailed, and you did not mourn.'"

Perhaps that's the best way of saying what some of us experience as the car door slams shut at the end of the drive and the evangelists walk toward the door. They will pipe and expect us to dance to their tune. It makes me want to run, or at least to pretend that I'm not at home. I cherish the gifts of God's grace. I fear people who would take away, by the violence of their unwavering demands, the more graceful kingdom that God has so quietly given.

It should be said that there are enthusiasts for things other than religion, and that they affect me in the same way. I knew a lady years ago who insisted that her home remedy would make me a better person, or at least a healthier one. The remedy consisted of blackstrap molasses, pepper, and honey. My excuses had about run out when, fortunately, I moved to another town.

If it isn't blackstrap molasses, it's Transcendental Meditation. I have nothing against T.M., and I have no doubt that it has been helpful to many. I just don't want to do it. One day I discovered in an airline magazine, buried in a column of trivia, a report that those who involve themselves in Transcendental Meditation, taken as a whole, have an above average tendency to depression. I tore it out and carried it in my briefcase for more than a year as defense against those who would have me dance the T.M. tune.

Now it's jogging and running. I'm sure that they are valuable, and I know that I should exercise regularly, but I prefer not to jog, and I run only for planes, where I scan the magazines for a report that such activity loosens the teeth, or whatever.

Sometimes, of course, the pressure to do things someone else's way is more intense than the pressure to try blackstrap molasses, T. M., or running.

One day a lady called me to ask what I was doing about world hunger. I thought I explained it well. Our office was responsible for the university-wide fast, which would not only provide information about hunger, but would also raise at least ten thousand dollars. She was not satisfied. A few days later I received a letter from the woman saying that if I really wanted to do something about world hunger, she'd be glad to have me join her group's efforts. I called her and explained again both our major and our minor hunger projects. "Well," she said, "I just don't feel that you are taking it seriously. What are you doing about the university faculty?" I was not smiling. I was not going to do anything about faculty members. They were enough informed to do something for themselves.

I admit, though, that this lady upset me. Am I doing enough? I look at the pictures of those living skeletons and find it hard to say the mealtime prayer over a modest supper. Am I not the rich young ruler, and before me Jesus saying that there is one more thing: that I sell what I have and give, give, give? But then it occurs to me that I'd rather be Zacchaeus. He agreed to give only half of what he had which, in many ways, seems not only more sensible, but more loving. If, in the early years of my earning an income and in each of the subsequent years of disasters and appeals, I had given everything, then someone else would have had to educate my children, house the refugees which we took in, care for me in sickness, and provide for me in declining years. And in all these years of living an ordinary life, I have, through taxes and the church, supported not only a family of five, but at least one other person, somewhere, as well. I feel like Saint Paul saying this, Saint Paul boasting of his trials. It's foolishness, and neither Saint Paul nor I intended to boast, but the lady who said I wasn't doing enough about world hunger got to me, didn't she? She made me defensive.

I really didn't want to take the blackstrap home remedy, do T.M., jog, or sell everything I have and give it all in relief of those suffering from the latest catastrophe. And I didn't. But I have a feeling that the real test will be the temptation to be converted, and I don't want to be converted.

Don't misunderstand. I do believe that Jesus Christ is my Lord and Savior. And part of that from which I am saved are the violent demands of those who say that I must do it their way.

I know when I was saved, too. It happened from the beginning when Adam and Eve, of love begotten, went astray, and we with them. Compassionate, God called out, searching. It happened one Friday afternoon, when long past demanding, the mangered Word stretched out his arms to draw to the heart of God a world gone wrong. It happened not long after I was born when believing parents brought me to the font, and I was drawn with Christ into death, and raised to a new life beyond demand and called John, one whom God has made his own, by love cradled and set free.

I don't want to be converted. I was in the terminal at La Guardia Airport one day looking at paperback books and hoping that two pilots would finish their conversation and move so that I could look where they were standing. When they didn't move, I reached around them. It turned out that one was evangelizing the other. "Jesus washed me clean," he said. "All the bad in me, the meanness, the evil thoughts, just drained right out of me. I gave up smoking . . . " I didn't hear any more, because I got out of there. I shouldn't be that way. After all, I too am a believer. I know that the pilot and I are brothers in Christ. But I am afraid that he will try to make me dance to the way he plays the tune.

The badness has not all drained out of me, nor all the meanness and evil thoughts. I'm sure he waits prayerfully for the guidance of God in his decision making, and for the most part I don't do that. God respects us enough to want us to make decisions for ourselves. And the pilot might just sell everything he has and give it to the hungry and expect me to do the same. His demand would make me feel guilty, and, if I actually did it, a little crazy. He probably is sure that abortion is always to be avoided as sinful. I know that it's contrary to the intention of God, but still, at times, an abortion is the course which love allows. He may well feel that we must strengthen our military forces against godless communism, or he may be a pacifist, and I'm not sure that either course is God's final word for every situation.

When we tell such people that we are Christians, they proceed to test our credentials. Graciously, of course, but we are nevertheless tested. Like all standard achievement tests, our success or failure, as they measure it, depends upon whether or not we use the language with which they are familiar. I know the traditional language of the evangelist, but prefer not to use it. I think I just don't want to be converted. Rather, I believe that one of the things from which I am already saved is the necessity of responding to a list of demands or requirements in order to be saved. John the Baptist, the man in the desert who had all the familiar marks of the holy man, eating locusts and wearing animal skins and preaching repentance, was said by Jesus to be among the least in the kingdom of heaven. This was not a put-down of John the Baptist. He was of the old order, as John the Baptist himself acknowledged. He said that he was not worthy to untie the shoelace of Christ. Why? Because Christ ushered in a new order, a time when we do not have to dance to the piper's tune or mourn when others wail. Our worth in the sight of God is not dependent upon meeting demands. Salvation is God's own compassionate gift and we are free to work out the meaning of that as best we can. We are free to acknowledge that we are not perfect, but imperfect people, deciding how much to give for world hunger and how much to spend for the needs of our own families, struggling to figure out whether an abortion is the answer which love requires or not, and having to live with the touch of meanness which won't simply drain away.

Does this mean that we are without guidance for our lives? Certainly not! Whether we understand the Ten Commandments to have been dictated by God on Sinai and brought down the mountain by Moses, or whether we understand them to have come in a less specific way out of the experience of the Jews as they interpreted the activity of the God they could not see, the commandments serve as bench marks describing the limits beyond which life in community becomes impossible. And there is more. Over the centuries faithful Jews and Christians have worked at the task of understanding the ways in which the law of God might reasonably be applied to the infinite variety of situations in which human beings find themselves. In addition, faithful Jews and Christians have tried to understand not only how the letter of the law applies to specific situations, but what the spirit of the law, the largest sense of it, might require.

It is this last effort, the work of discerning the spirit of the law, for which Jesus Christ is praised by those of us who follow him. He said that the whole law could be summarized in two interrelated commandments. We are to love the Lord our God above all else, and our neighbors as ourselves. And that makes many people uneasy. When a person lies for months in a coma and the best-informed opinion is that the person will not recover consciousness, then the fifth commandment says that this life cannot be taken. The command to love our neighbor may suggest another course of action. Sometimes the simplicities of an authoritative answer are so attractive that we cling to them long past the time when they serve as guides and tempt us instead to abrogate the responsibilities of mature faith. The meaning of love must ultimately be forged in the crucible of decision.

I know that the people who stop at the bottom of the drive

and walk toward the house with Bible in hand are well intentioned, and that they prayed before they started out. I honor their commitment and the cause which they serve. They are, nevertheless, piping a tune to which I will not dance. I am by grace already a child of God, embraced by a love beyond demands. "From the days of John the Baptist until now the kingdom of heaven has suffered violence, and men of violence take it by force."

"[The prodigal son] arose and came to his father. But while he was yet at a distance, his father saw him and had compassion, and ran and embraced him and kissed him. And the son said to him, 'Father, I have sinned against heaven and before you; I am no longer worthy to be called your son.' But the father said to his servants, 'Bring quickly the best robe, and put it on him; and put a ring on his hand, and shoes on his feet; and bring the fatted calf and kill it, and let us eat and make merry; for this my son was dead, and is alive again; he was lost, and is found.' "

Luke 15:20–24

5 | *Ring, Robe, and Shoes*

The parable of the prodigal son is so simple and direct that it has become a part of the folklore of Western culture. A son takes his inheritance, departs for a far country, and squanders his money in riotous living (KJV). It doesn't work out, of course, and, penitent, the prodigal returns to a loving father who rejoices that this son has come to his senses and welcomes him back with a party. Good triumphs over evil, and that's the way God intends that it should be.

What is not said and what most of us don't understand until we've been around awhile is that there is a price to be paid for being forgiven as the prodigal was—a cost for wearing the father's ring, robe, and shoes. We don't always leave home because we are bad persons who enjoy riotous living. Sometimes we go to far countries to escape the love which bestows such gifts.

Our leave-takings are many. Years ago, there were fields surrounding the Cleveland Airport, and we lived there in a house later destroyed to make room for airport parking. But at that time, the land grew timothy, clover, wild strawberries, and wild asters, and was home for meadowlarks and red-winged blackbirds. I often went to that far country, to pick strawberries, I said, but mostly to flatten down some of the tall grass and make a private place where I could lie on my back and see the blue sky and listen to the larks.

We had a tree house, too, made of boards and burlap, and over on the next road some friends had dug a bunker underground, lit with bits of candles. We had homes, all of us, and rooms, usually shared with a brother or sister. But homes belonged to parents, and rooms were invaded for cleaning and making the bed, and treasures had to be hidden. To be free, there had to be a place which was our own, a hiding place. Is it really any different now?

People also go to far countries for economic reasons. Things were not going well in Palestine at the time this parable was told, and four million Jews had already gone to other places, just as millions of Irish left their homeland when the potato harvests failed. Moreover, younger sons received a smaller inheritance than elder sons, and in some countries, like daughters everywhere, younger sons received nothing at all.

But it's a reasonable guess that the younger son didn't leave because he was a bad person, or for economic reasons, but out of a desire for independence—the longing to be free of the weight of established ways of doing things, of expectations framed by long tradition. Even in our maturity, many of us long for freedom from such expectations and consider early retirement, not because we want to sit, but because, whatever we do, we'd like to do it at times and under circumstances of our own choosing.

Whether for economic reasons, in search of independence, or something of both, the younger son took his journey to a far country where two things happened. (There's seldom one thing that happens.) The first was his riotous living. That was his responsibility, and he had to own that. The second thing which happened was a famine in that place. He was not responsible for the famine. The combination of the two did him in, and, close to starving, he decided to go home.

The candles in the underground bunker eventually went out, and those children went home; those in the tree house and the boy on his back looking at the sky, they all went home too. Most of us do in one way or another; usually because we, like the prodigal, are starving. Americans in large numbers plan trips to Europe, not because they were born in Sweden, Germany, or Italy, or even that their parents were born there, but because a long time ago these countries were home. So is the ancestral farm, and we take our children there, stopping beside the road to tell them the familiar myths of origin. It's the same for the old grade school and town where we grew up, the college or university we attended, the place where we lived when our children were born. Black Americans wonder if they have a home at all, and they miss it. "Roots," we call them now. There are many ways of starving, and there are many ways of going home.

There is integrity in the way the prodigal framed his speech to his father. He could have said, "In part because of a famine over which I had no control, I was forced to return." He chose instead the harder part, the riotous living. "Father, I have sinned against heaven and before you; I am no longer worthy to be called your son."

Actually, he had planned to say more than that. He had rehearsed it. "Treat me as one of your hired servants." We usually have something that we plan to offer. It would be too humiliating otherwise. "I'm starving, but your servants are eating, so I ask forgiveness and a chance to earn my meals as they do." Silas, the returnee in Robert Frost's "Death of the Hired Man," had a plan, too—something to offer when he returned. He would clear the upper meadow spring and teach the neighbor boy how to build a load of hay. The wayward husband, when he returns home, has a plan to treat the children better and to spend more time around the house. We have a plan, too, when we return to God. We will do what we can to make up for the damage we've done and try not to repeat our offenses. We have a plan.

Now the father did the best he could—the best and the worst. He had compassion, ran down the road, and embraced the younger son. In some ways, his behavior was magnificent. He did not stand and wait so that the son would see him there and have to face that quarter mile of walking toward his judgment. The answer was given in the first seeing of one another. There was no silence while the son stammered out the words of penitence, and then the embrace. The son's penitence was offered within the embrace already given, which was the father's yes to a question not yet asked. There was no reasoned discourse, no sorting out the riotous living which was blameworthy from the famine which was not, followed by lawyer-careful condemnation. There was only the ring, the robe, and the shoes, the sound of music and the meal of celebration. It was the best the father could do. It is the way, said Jesus, that God welcomes us home. The father did the best that he could, and the worst.

Why the worst? Because it left so little place for the prodigal's selfhood, for his sense of freedom and independence. How could the son do his fair share in this kind of reconciliation? Even his request to be received came after the answer had been given. He could not even pay by receiving the blows of his father's silence or condemnation. He could not work out the reconciliation by being a servant for a time and earning a new place in the household. It was worse than that. Instead of paying something for his return, he received the symbolic gifts of the ring, the robe, and the shoes. He was left not a shred of self-justification while the music played, his friends gathered, and the flames crackled under the turning spit.

"Love at its best," the Sunday school teachers said. But some thoughtful people hold back and will not be loved like that, forgiven and received like that. It's embarrassing to come so empty-handed. Even as children when we went home from the tree house, it was to serve out our tutelage until the time when we were old enough to leave again and be truly independent. Even for serious Christians, it is not enough to give to God our prayer, praise, and thanksgiving. Our hands are filled with gifts. For some it may be years of service in the church, offered like a bottle of wine to the host. For others of us it may be a family well reared, some job well done. It seems more appropriate that way, and far less embarrassing than coming with nothing and being totally dependent upon the graciousness of God.

It was not surprising when, some years ago, a group of theologians declared the death of God, and praised him for shuffling off the world's stage of his own accord so that our freedom might be complete. "God," they said, "just by being

God, by his very loving us, is the ultimate enemy of our freedom and sense of independence. If he is truly loving, he must set us free of himself, of his very presence."

The father did his best, but for those who choose independence, who prefer for dignity's sake to pay their own way, it was the worst. The gifts of ring, robe, and shoes gave shape to a new bondage.

How shall we escape? We would much prefer a contract, which is the way we've learned to live successfully and with some dignity in the world of every day. We make arrangements. The son or daughter who returns from the secluded place in the field agrees to do the things required of minors. Parents accept accountability for paying taxes, housing and feeding children, and leaving a telephone number where they can be reached when they go out at night. We know that we were not made to be solitary, and that to live with others requires justice in our giving and taking. We balance our needs against our responsibilities. We spend a third of the day working for others and balance it by taking time for ourselves. We balance our time being parents with our time as lovers, service to the commonwealth with our desire to walk in the woods. We keep a balance of good works against our shortcomings—those things which we know please God against those things which we sense to be violations of his design.

But sometimes this ordered world becomes radically disordered. An act of adultery is discovered which completely unbalances years of faithfulness. There are the critical days when we discover that a youthful dream is dead and cannot ever be revived, the day when we recognize our complicity in a great slaughter, a prejudice long denied, a status in the eyes of others totally different than we had led ourselves to believe. Sometimes our neatly balanced world of contract utterly collapses and we hold nothing in our hands at all.

When our world of contract ends and we go home to God with only darkness in our hands, we usually go with a plan. We will clear the meadow spring, work as servants in our father's house, or somehow make it up to those we've hurt. The meaning of this parable is that our plan will go unspoken, God's embrace will precede our showing of the darkness, and we will receive the ring, the robe, and the shoes.

The parable does not tell us about the feelings of the prodigal who returns under these conditions. Logic and our own experience, together with the witness of many others, tell us that to be loved by God in this way means inevitably a total surrender of the self and an end to our dreams of independence.

It's true that within this embrace of love, there is no humiliation. There is, nevertheless, the evocation of the ultimate humility. We are not galley slaves, but it is God's ring, robe, and shoes that we wear. The parable is good news for the mature not because it sets us totally free or restores the life of contract which usually serves us well, but because we are taken captive by the love of God revealed in Jesus Christ, rather than by other loves.

We've all been told that we must love ourselves if we are to love others, that self-affirmation is the beginning of our freedom. And there are times when we are capable of saying, "I'm all right, a valuable person, and able to do things." There are two times when this is actually easy. One of them is in the afterglow of some accomplishment, the successful completion of a project, or a successful competition. The other is at the moment that someone tells us we must affirm ourselves, though one suspects that what makes self-love possible at that moment is that the other person is, in fact, affirming us by telling us to affirm ourselves.

There are other times when it is not easy or even possible to love ourselves. These are the times when, like the prodigal son, we have behaved in ways which make us ashamed or, more profoundly, the times of great loneliness when we drift through immense space where no one calls our name or even sees us floating there. These are the times of our greatest suffering. By what miracle or magic words will we at these times be able to love ourselves?

Being seen by others is the warrant for the knowledge that we exist. Being affirmed by others is the warrant for our affirmation that our existence is important. Being loved by others is what makes it possible for us to love ourselves. To be this dependent upon other human beings is threatening. What is given can be taken away, and we wax or wane with this giving and receiving of recognition and love.

When we, like the prodigal, go home to God, are embraced by God, and receive the ring, the robe, and the shoes, we become the servants of God, dependent upon him for the establishment and maintenance of our meaning and worth. Can God be trusted with our life in his hands? Countless others, out of their experience, answer yes. But in the end, it is your experience, and my own, which really matters.

"Now his elder son was in the field; and as he came and drew near to the house, he heard music and dancing. And he called one of the servants and asked what this meant. And he said to him 'Your brother has come, and your father has killed the fatted calf, because he has received him safe and sound.' But he was angry and refused to go in. His father came out and entreated him, but he answered his father, 'Lo, these many years I have served you, and I never disobeyed your command; yet you never gave me a kid, that I might make merry with my friends. But when this son of yours came, who has devoured your living with harlots, you killed for him the fatted calf!' And he said to him, 'Son, you are always with me, and all that is mine is yours. It was fitting to make merry and be glad, for this your brother was dead, and is alive; he was lost, and is found.' "

Luke 15:25–32

6 | *The Elder Son's Defense*

To All Concerned for Justice:

Greetings!

Year after year preachers great and small, in a hundred languages, lead you from the bathos of my younger brother's self-imposed exile to the sounds of dancing and leave you staring at me, disgusted because I will not share the celebration for the prodigal's return. It's time that you heard my side of the story, what it's like to be an elder brother and why I reacted as I did.

I should, I suppose, enlist the aid of a panel of experts. My brother has, after all, turned his case over to the worthy clergy who have so embroidered their bias in his favor that I can never hope to balance the facts by myself. It occurs to me, however, that many of the people of the world are themselves elder brothers, and, I hasten to add, elder sisters, and that our common status will facilitate a larger understanding. So I make my own defense in the hope that a simple, honest statement is all that's needed.

I cannot deny that one unlovely moment in my life to which the clergy point. I had come from the fields at evening, as has been reported, and when I heard the sound of dancing and smelled the roasting meat I was surprised and asked a servant what was happening. I cannot deny the jealousy and hurt which rose within me when I learned that it was a party for my wayward brother. I make no defense for my behavior. I cannot even say that I would behave differently should history repeat itself. But I want you to understand that I will regret it for the rest of my life. I hate the feeling in myself. I know that jealousy is the worst of me.

Without in any way defending my reaction, I do want to say what it's like to be an elder brother. I think you'll understand, and I need that understanding.

Let me say first of all that being an elder brother has something to do with being responsible. I'm not referring to chronological age, but about an elder brother syndrome which can occur in the life of anyone. And the most significant element in the elder brother syndrome is a sense of responsibility.

I was responsible for a large farm. We had servants, of course, lots of them, but there is a difference between being a servant and being an owner. Servants take orders, but owners are the ones who take responsibility. We are the ones who must decide when the fields are ready to plow and plant. We select the seed. Owners decide how many sheep the land can support. We decide when to shear the sheep. And since there will inevitably be bad years when the crops fail and the sheep die, it is our responsibility to see that enough food and money has been set aside so that the farm can continue and the servants be fed.

Do you think that I had no moments—even days, weeks, months—when I wanted to leave? That I have no hunger for wine, women, and song? Do you think I was born a drudge? No, I was born an elder brother, son of aging parents who looked to me to share the responsibility of being an owner. From the day I was born I was reared to be accountable, as though my parents, the servants, and all the generations to follow were dependent upon me. I was reared to be responsible. I say this with only a touch of pride, certainly not with regret. I say it only in the hope that you will understand me.

There are those who come to a party, and there are those who work to prepare for that party, who see to it that the house is clean, that there is enough wine, that the fire is well built, and that the musicians are ready. There are those who go home from the party singing their happy songs, and there are those of us who clean up after them, who sweep the cracker crumbs and bits of smoked fish from the floor and wipe the white circles left by the mugs on the polished wood. There are those who come as guests and go home carefree, and there are those who prepare for the party and clean up when the revelry is over. I am one of the latter, you see. Usually, I am not unhappy about this, nor offensively proud of it either. It's one of the roles in the human family, and I play it well. I am marked with the elder brother syndrome.

Let me say also that elder brothers are harder to love. I wonder sometimes why it is that people find it so easy to love people like my younger brother. (Notice that now I call him my brother. It was only in that awful moment of jealousy when the worst of me came out that I called him my father's younger son.) His offenses were so clear. He had wasted money which had come from generations of work on the farm. He had lived with harlots. He came home with nothing. Why is it so easy to accept the wayward? Perhaps they are so vulnerable that it's easy to accept them. They are so obviously in trouble that they pose no threat. Perhaps it's easiest to love people who are no threat — the fools, those who write their sinning large.

I have been pictured as self-righteous, the hardest of all to love. I know that. But look into your own hearts, you elder brothers and sisters, those of you who, like me, are responsible. You know that we are sinners, too. I work with the servants in the field, and as the sun grows unbearably hot, my anger rises and I find myself beating the ground so hard with the hoe that the handle breaks. The other day the goat kicked over the pail of milk again and, in anger, I kicked the goat. You laugh, perhaps, but it is of the nature of elder brothers and sisters to carry their anger, their sins, hidden within their hearts. What did you expect? Should I go home and say to my father, "Father, I have sinned against heaven and against you. Today I was angry and broke another hoe, and yesterday I kicked a goat?"

No, elder brothers and sisters are the responsible kind, and our sins are not obvious nor easily shared. Therefore, we are harder to love.

I want also to acknowledge that being responsible has its rewards. I do understand that my father was right when he said, "You are always with me and all that is mine is yours." I know that, I really do. My satisfaction, the reward for my being responsible, is to look out over a field sprouting green and to take in the beauty of it and, in the harvest, to gather in the sheaves, exulting in the weight of the sacks of grain filled from the threshing floor. My reward is that of a job well done, of a household running smoothly with people fed and with provision against the times of famine, and the taxes paid. My satisfaction is in the respect of those around me, in being able to give to those in need. I am a gold watch person. We elder brothers and sisters, we are the ninety and nine who take care of ourselves, the ones whom the shepherd can leave to look for the lost.

As you can tell, I write these words easily. I know what our rewards are, coming quietly every day of our lives. But it is so hard to see that no-good son of my father . . . . Excuse me. It is so hard to see my younger brother come home empty-handed and receive the ring, the robe, and the shoes, to smell the roasting meat and hear the music for his dancing. Ah, the anger is not all gone, is it? I understand it with my mind and I know how to say it with words, that elder brothers are responsible and sinners like everyone else, the harder to love, whose rewards come quietly day by day. Gold watch people. I understand it. It's harder to make my emotions behave.

Well, that's my side of the story. But I leave you with a question. How shall we be saved, we elder brothers and sisters? How can we go home when we are already home? How can we confess the squandering of resources, the harlots, the months and years of neglect, when in fact we have built and not squandered, not gone with harlots, and been responsible for preserving the family fortunes? How shall we be helped: those of us with our secret anger and the harlotry which stays in our hearts; those of us who are hard to love because we show so little need, who show only on rare occasions the jealousy which made me turn away from the dancing to become forever the ill-reputed elder brother? How shall we be saved?

I'll tell you what I think, and you may have some insight too. It would probably help if we shared with others some of the responsibilities which make our lives such a burden. Do we have to be owners in the sense that we make all of the decisions?

Wouldn't it make for a less lonely and isolated life if we invited our servants to be partners in the productive process? Teachers and students could become collaborators in the process of gaining and sharing knowledge. Managers and those they now manage could become partners in a common enterprise. Children could share more of the responsibilities for creating a family, and by that I mean that children could help to make decisions and not simply respond to shouted orders. Do we not, by the very way in which we structure our relationships, create the burdens under which we chafe and grow angry? To become less owner-like, to enter into partnerships and to be collaborators — that could be a part of our salvation.

I suppose that this could be said in a less pompous way. (It has probably not escaped your attention that self-importance is one of the more obvious manifestations of the elder brother syndrome.) You'll remember that, among other things, I said to my father, "You never gave me a kid, that I might make merry with my friends." The truth of the matter is that I never asked my father if I could have a party. I wonder about that. Somehow it didn't seem appropriate. There was always so much to do, not just with my hands — that's the easy part — but so much thinking to be done, so many problems to be solved. Thinking and problem solving don't mix with parties. Actually, I think I was concerned about the appearance of things. Would the servants and the neighbors look up to a person, depend upon a person who throws a party, drinks wine, and dances? A cocktail before dinner is one thing, but a party?

To be perfectly honest, I don't have many friends. I'm respected, you understand. When I go to the bank, the teller calls me sir and my check is never refused. I like that. But there is a difference between respect and friendship. So you see, by assuming authority and by refusing to share it, I have set myself apart. I have fit myself into a total model of human interaction in which I have isolated myself and must behave according to the model. I never asked my father for a kid so that I might make merry with my friends. Servants and prodigals dance. I have a drink before dinner. Servants and prodigals have friends. I have respect. Isn't there some other model for elder brothers? That's my question and a larger sharing of responsibility could well be a part of the answer.

Another part of our salvation could be a fuller recognition of the gifts which come to us day by day as a consequence of our being responsible. If we could see more often the greening fields which we have planted and know our partnership with God; if we could see our growing children fed and clothed and rejoice in our partnership with them and with God; if we could rejoice to feed the hungry, to set some tangled person free — then we would probably find in these things a quiet joy which is both our reward and a replacement for our anger. This would be a part of our salvation. My father said it well, "Son, you are always with me, and all that is mine is yours." And will our heavenly Father deny us this healing sense of partnership with him if we ask that he renew a right spirit within us?

The other part of our salvation must be the same as that experienced by our younger brothers and sisters, the prodigals. Our sins are not flamboyant; in many ways they are a little boring, but no less damaging. In fact our hidden anger may be more damaging than their more flagrant sins, at least to those around us. In some ways it would be easier to repent of what is obvious, the extravagant sins of the far country, than to speak the pain of our jealousy and self-righteousness, the hidden anger and dark fantasies which come as we pursue our more ordered lives.

God knows these hidden sins, of course. Erect, we stand as solid citizens before the cross, but our hearts are bowed; he embraces us with his eyes, and not just those who are bent with weeping. There may be no turning spit and no music for dancing. We the elder are not the best of dancers anyway. But we go down the hill from Golgotha knowing that he died for us, too. We go down to our green valley to see the field of sprouting seed, knowing that all that he has is ours, and we are his.

O God, creator of the elder brothers and sisters of the world,
   have mercy on us.

O God, redeemer of those unmasked by a moment of jealousy,
   have mercy on us.
O God, sustainer of those who receive gold watches,
   grant us your peace.

Pilate then called together the chief priests and the rulers and the people, and said to them, "You brought me this man as one who was perverting the people; and after examining him before you, behold, I did not find this man guilty of any of your charges against him; neither did Herod, for he sent him back to us. Behold, nothing deserving death has been done by him; I will therefore chastise him and release him."

But they all cried out together, "Away with this man, and release to us Barabbas"—a man who had been thrown into prison for an insurrection started in the city, and for murder. . . .

And as they led him away, they seized one Simon of Cyrene, who was coming in from the country, and laid on him the cross, to carry it behind Jesus. . . .

Now there was a man named Joseph from the Jewish town of Arimathea. He was a member of the council, a good and righteous man, who had not consented to their purpose and deed, and he was looking for the kingdom of God. This man went to Pilate and asked for the body of Jesus. Then he took it down and wrapped it in a linen shroud, and laid him in a rock-hewn tomb, where no one had ever yet been laid.

Luke 23:13–19, 26, 50–53

7 | *At the Edge*

It is hard to avoid religion when you live in a culture where you are surrounded by believing people. "We always start our meetings with prayer," said the owner of a small taxicab company in New York City. Cab drivers? If business executives and members of Congress can have prayer breakfasts, and football players can pray in the huddle, why not? Even if one manages to avoid such occasions, it won't be long before a wedding, funeral, or "christening" will mandate a trip to church or temple. Actually, we handle these events quite well. It's a matter of being unobtrusive and watching someone who seems to know what they are doing.

There are other situations which are more perplexing. They arise when our normal routine is broken, when a wife or husband is away for a week, or when some unusual event occurs which reorders our lives; a tragedy within the family, perhaps. These experiences may result from becoming immersed in a book like Walker Percy's *The Second Coming,* or the arrival on our scene of a strong and unusual person. Whatever the occasion, the consequence is that we find ourselves pondering a mystery we didn't know existed. It's as though the working answers to our questions of identity and purpose have fallen out of place, and we have to pick up the pieces and put them together again. It's not that we've had a conversion experience —far from it. But we have certainly received an invitation to reconsider.

There were three people who had this kind of experience as a result of a chance inclusion in the trial, death, and burial of Jesus of Nazareth. They just happened to be there: Barabbas in prison, Simon of Cyrene walking into town at the wrong time, and Joseph of Arimathea serving on the court before which Jesus had been brought. They were at the edge of a major drama in human history. Like most things human, their experience was not much different from our own, though the details of the occasion vary.

We don't know much about Barabbas except that he was an insurrectionist and a murderer. It's easier to think that the murder occurred in the struggle to free his land from tyranny. While all killing is to be feared, murder in the cause of justice is at least comprehensible. There is no reason to believe that Barabbas ever saw Jesus, heard him, or talked with him. Their tie to one another was accidental. It just so happened that Pontius Pilate, the Roman procurator before whom Jesus was brought after his arrest, found no crime for which he should be punished. The crowd was disappointed and became ugly. Pilate remembered that at this time of year a prisoner was normally released, a clever device to mollify the dissidents among a captive people. If the crowd would accept the release of Jesus, the matter was settled. The crowd preferred Barabbas, as they would anywhere — a political revolutionary to a religious man whose teachings meant a change too close to home. So Barabbas was released and melded with the crowd on his way to freedom, while Jesus was pushed toward the cross.

Nothing is written in the biblical texts concerning how Barabbas felt about his escape. Novelists like Par Lagerkvist have written what they assume he felt; most of us can imagine it, too. We have also been released while another died. An airline flight is missed because of an accident on the interstate, and those who made the flight died in a crash. There is a fire in a hotel, but we are not there because we arrived too late and they gave our room to someone else. Why was I born an American, in a family which read books and cherished education, that cared when I came in at night? What right have I to eat while others starve, to be warm while others shiver out the winter, to have credit while others are turned away?

Barabbas was not the first nor the last to stand in some bright place and see grief surround another, and to wonder why he deserved to be so free.

Sometimes we know the answer. We may have worked harder, been more honest, or patiently built a pattern of life which produced good things. But just as often, there is no correlation. It would help if we could say, as some of the faithful do, that God sent us good fortune, that God so rules and governs our lives that we are shielded and protected. Some of us reject instinctively any god who would arbitrarily assign good things to us while depriving others. It also offends our every day observation to believe that good is always rewarded and evil always punished. Life, as we experience it, is more complex.

How did Barabbas understand his unexpected freedom? We don't know. There are enough clues in our own experience, though, to imagine some of what he must have felt.

There is usually a sense of relationship and indebtedness to those who suffer instead of us. Even though it be an unintended substitution, or even accidental, there is a feeling that we have our good things at the expense of someone else, and that we owe it to the dead, the poor, the cold, hungry, and helpless people of the world to use our gifts well.

Some of us call it stewardship, and it has nothing at all to do with condescension toward the helpless or even with being a good or kindly person. It means that much of what we have doesn't really belong to us. We just happen to have it by virtue of some accident of birth or by being in the right place at the right time. Our joy in what we have depends in part upon responsible use of what we have. Why do some of us feel this way about it and others not at all?

Another experience is that of profound gratitude, a desire to give thanks to someone even when we're not sure that there was a giver of the gift. Time and again on the "Evening News," people who don't seem particularly pious at all say things like, "I'm just grateful to God for being alive" or "I thank Almighty God for leading me to the right place." Whether or not there is a source of our good fortune, many of us feel a need to give thanks. Gratitude in search of a name is central to religious experience.

When you meet persons like Barabbas — and it may be yourself — though they attend no church and make no confession that Jesus Christ is Lord, you meet persons at the edge of faith. They hold in their hands a wonder, an accident of release which they understand as a gift — a man or a woman who senses an indebtedness to others who did not escape, who is inclined toward a stewardship of the gifts of life and in search of a name to use in the giving of thanks.

The second person who is accidentally involved in the death of Jesus is Simon of Cyrene. We know little about him too, except that he was coming in from the country and was forced to help Jesus carry his cross. Tradition says that he was black, and that makes sense. He was easy to spot as being neither Jew nor Roman, and was one who therefore could be ordered to perform a dirty job. Or he may have been a strong country boy, a little taller than the rest, uncomfortable in city streets — an obvious choice. We know how these things happen: the not-too-bright girls cajoled and flattered into prostitution, the "go-fer" in the office who is easily made the butt of jokes and playfully coerced into doing what others rise above. He is the immigrant who doesn't know the language or the ways, who needs a start, who is drawn into the mines and factories, and who purchases dearly at the company store.

Simon was probably not angry or indignant at being forced to carry the cross. For such people, and they are legion, such abuse is no surprise, and there is no escape. Before him there had been galley slaves and builders of pyramids and after him would come impressed seamen, indentured servants, sweatshops, and battered wives.

What a world! Is there no hope? Has it always been the same and will it be so until the end of time, one generation after another of Simons forced to carry crosses while their teeth fall out and their children grow dull-eyed from hunger? Of women walking the streets in fear of a world in which they are powerless, even over their own bodies; people who are always suspect just because they are poor, objects of condescension, charity and welfare, the butt of ethnic jokes, forced to build fences which wall them out from the larger world of justice where worth and dignity are a right to be expected?

What's so amazing is that the answer was being forged in the drama in which Simon was forced to be a part. We don't know whether he believed that or not or had even heard the claim that in this Jesus, God was creating hope for people like himself.

Some things were different this time. It was not a rich man's burden that Simon was forced to carry. He carried the cross of a man badly beaten himself, too weak to walk with the weight. This Jesus was a gentle man, a working man, not much to look at, but a healer of the sick and a giver of gifts who never demeaned those he helped in the process of helping them. He was a man who refused to build fences, as much an insurrectionist as Barabbas; a man who didn't deserve to die and though crucified, dead and buried, was raised on the third day. Perhaps Simon heard that rumor. If there is any hope for the Simons of the world, any hope for blacks, country boys, galley slaves, immigrants, "go-fers," and battered women, that hope does not rest in us, in those with power, those of us secure within our privileged compounds. The future of the oppressed is in their own hands. But they will make this their future only if they have hope themselves—only if they believe that God, some god, is alive and powerfully at work in this world raising the dead, redressing the balance of justice, establishing what is true, and rebuilding ruined cities.

Whether the Simons of the world have hope for a different future, enough hope to fight for change, depends in large measure on whether they encounter the risen Christ alive, reordering, and making free on the streets where they live. And the risen Christ will not be wearing a long white robe. He will be hidden in the hearts of ordinary people who are convinced that the power and love of God did not end on Calvary, and who are determined to live by the promises of God and to set those promises against present realities. Whether the Simons of the

world can hope for change depends in large part on whether the
baptized people of the churches live out the meaning of the
resurrection. It must be one of the greatest risks God ever took.

The third person to become embroiled in the death of Jesus
was Joseph of Arimathea, a Jewish town. We do know
something about him in contrast to our lack of knowledge
about Barabbas and Simon of Cyrene, probably because he was
higher on the social ladder. We know that he was a member of
the Sanhedrin, one of the seventy-one priests, scribes, and
elders who sat in judgment over the keeping of the law. We
know that Joseph was one of those who had voted in the
minority when Jesus was brought before the Sanhedrin. He may
have been a disciple of Jesus, but that seems unlikely. He is
reported to have been a good man, open and waiting for the
coming of the kingdom of God. We know that it was because of
him that Jesus' body was not left on the cross. He went to Pilate
and asked permission to remove it, which was granted, and he
wrapped it in linen and laid it in a new tomb hewn from rock.

Life is easier if we can keep things simple. It's easier if
everyone can be divided into good people and bad people, the
saved and the unsaved, the rich who are sent empty away and
the poor who are raised up, the religious professionals who op-
pose Jesus and the common people who support him. Like it or
not, Joseph doesn't fit this simple model. A member of the
religious ruling class, he nevertheless voted a minority opinion
when Jesus came before his court. A man of substance who, in
simplism's categories, should have been a bad person, he per-
formed a gracious and humane act. Thoroughly establishment,
he was not intimidated by a challenge to the institution which
he helped to rule.

There are more of such people than we sometimes suppose. A
secretary of state resigns because his conscience cannot condone
the risks of a military effort to rescue hostages. An engineer
resigns because he believes the product his company manufac-
tures is unsafe. A young woman "with a promising future" goes
to Nepal to help villagers install water pipes. A black medical
student who could earn a fortune in a northeastern city chooses

to practice in the small southern town where he almost died because there was no doctor for black people.

All around us are men and women who are principled, thoughtful, and open to the kingdom of God. They are people who are not afraid to go to Pilate and ask for the body of Jesus. Sometimes their high position intimidates us, and it would never occur to us to talk with them about the things to which both of us may be committed. They don't easily fit our simple categories of bad and good, and we find that confusing. Like Joseph of Arimathea, they stand at the edge of the Passion narrative and thoughtfully do what is appropriate. Whether, at some final accounting, they are among the saved is for God to decide. Whether, in the time which is now, they become a part of the community of praise and thanksgiving, receiving the bread and the wine, depends in part upon the capacity of church people to live beyond simple categories.

> Barabbas, a man set free, become indebted, and in search of someone to thank.
> Simon of Cyrene, one of the oppressed, bearing a cross which is to become the source of the hope which is essential to change in his life.
> Joseph of Arimathea, a man secure enough to vote against his social class and looking for the kingdom of God.

These three entered by happenstance into the trial and death of Jesus and are now among us as tens of thousands, people touched in some way by the gospel. They invite us to share their experience and insight and wait, perhaps, for a witness from the people of Christ concerning the meaning of what they have experienced and for a word of invitation.

No doubt at those countless points where the worlds of believers and those at the edge overlap, the Holy Spirit is at work calling those who believe to some larger risk, those at the edge to public discipleship – and waiting to reveal to all of us a peace which is more profound than that which any of us have imagined.

But on the first day of the week, at early dawn, they went to the tomb, taking the spices which they had prepared. And they found the stone rolled away from the tomb, but when they went in they did not find the body. . . .

That very day two of them were going to a village named Emmaus, about seven miles from Jerusalem, and talking with each other about all these things that had happened. While they were talking and discussing together, Jesus himself drew near and went with them. But their eyes were kept from recognizing him. . . .

So they drew near to the village to which they were going. He appeared to be going further, but they constrained him, saying, "Stay with us, for it is toward evening and the day is now far spent." So he went in to stay with them. When he was at table with them, he took the bread and blessed, and broke it, and gave it to them. And their eyes were opened and they recognized him; and he vanished out of their sight.

Luke 24:1–3, 13–16, 28–31

8 | *Nighttime City Street*

Majestic lives which end hideously may provide us with examples of how to die with dignity, but who would call such deaths good news? It's awesome to contemplate a God who by incarnation suffers death on behalf of his creation, but if the witness ends with "crucified, dead, and buried," then that's not good news either. It simply means that nothing much has changed and that even God was finally overcome by the ultimate enemy: death.

It is clear from New Testament writings that the first followers of Jesus probably didn't expect him to die at the hands of the Romans. How could Messiah die? It is also clear that once dead, they expected that to be the end of it. They were not out there in the garden waiting for angels to roll away the stone. What some of them experienced was a double reversal. The one who could not die died, and then the one who was dead appeared alive among them. It's no wonder that there was a lot of confusion concerning the meaning of it all. In fact, the confusion continues. One thing became clear. Not everything was what it seemed to be. If God could, in Jesus, suffer death, and if Jesus was raised from the dead, then death was not the ultimate victor and all kinds of reversals were possible. That is good news with multiple implications.

One of the implications is that to whatever extent you believe that Jesus was raised from the dead, just to that extent there is delight in the reversals which are encountered in odd ways and times throughout our lives. Moreover, the believer understands these experiences of reversal as the everyday outworking of the resurrection paradigm.

Such an event happened in front of our house in the center of the city, the only single family house in the downtown area still used as a residence. The study windows, large and set in heavy moldings, provide a constantly changing scene. One night the scene was a young woman walking rapidly past the house and followed by a car. The driver was talking to her, or shouting. Two students going in the opposite direction paused as though concerned. The woman hurried on and the car kept pace, clearly following her. The students would have helped, but had no haven to offer. Leaving my own door ajar so I wouldn't be locked out, I ran to catch up with her, and then slowed so that she wouldn't be frightened by my approach. "Can I help?" I asked. "Would you like to use my telephone?" She paused, not sure of me and not quite understanding. I repeated the offer of assistance. The car had turned around and was coming toward us. Then a warm smile appeared on her dark face and she relaxed. "Thank you so much," she said, "but the people in the car are my friends and we are just looking for number fifty-six on this street."

This is one way of saying what Easter means in the Christian experience of the world. It is the warm smile of a dark face on a nighttime city street. It is surprise at being so wrong concerning someone we had every right to expect to be just one more frightened person.

Easter is a group of women who gathered spices and ointments and walked to a burial place to prepare a body, only to discover that the body was not there. Easter is two people walking the road to Emmaus, lamenting the death of one called Jesus. A stranger joined them, and they talked about their shattered hope. When they came to the house where the two of them lived, they invited the third to join them for supper because it was evening and the day had come to its close. The guest took the bread, broke it, gave thanks, and disappeared. The two rose and ran back to Jerusalem where, exhausted, they told the disciples about the reversal which had occurred at their table.

Easter is to be surprised by life at times and places where all of our previous experience has prepared us to expect death.

"Just give us a simple rule to follow," some say. "We will walk in the steps of the Master." That would at least let some of us bypass the hard-to-believe doctrine of the resurrection. But the footsteps of Jesus always end at the cross and, eventually, the constant ending up at the cross becomes depressing. That's what happened to the people who immersed themselves in the social gospel in the early part of the century. They intended to build the kingdom of God by following the example of Jesus. The people of the social gospel died of heartache induced by wars and the Great Depression of the 1930s. If following in the footsteps of Jesus is all that the church has to say, it would be better left unsaid so that people can be uninhibited in their fight to survive as long as possible.

Granted, to make commitment to the resurrection of Christ is an act of faith, and there is no proof to facilitate such a commitment. But the vitality of Christianity and what makes it at least interesting is the doctrine, the teaching, that however human beings in their God-given freedom choose to abuse themselves and one another, we cannot take the compassion of God, hang it on a cross, lay it in a tomb, and expect to find it there three days later when we come to give it proper burial. The faithful one is betrayed, the man of peace is beaten, the healer dies, and they lay him in a tomb. It happens all the time. That is normal, and it's why the students and I were sure that the people in the car were harrassing the woman walking the sidewalk. It happens all the time.

What does not happen all the time is to find the tomb empty or, when day is over, to recognize the risen Christ in the breaking of bread. What does not happen all the time is the reversal of what is usual: an empty tomb or a smile instead of harrassment on a nighttime city street.

To be a follower of Jesus and do life his way by walking in his steps — that is open to anyone with the will to try. The footsteps end at death, of course. But the excitement and possibility central to the teaching of the church, that which is sometimes known to faith or is to be longed for, is that the Christ who was dead has been raised, and that death is not the ultimate victor. It is the conviction that what has been need not always be, not because we are good enough or moral enough to change the world, but because God has no intention of allowing our lives to be that dull. Easter is the witness that we are saved from more of the same by the experience of the unexpected.

If we come with our spices to prepare the body and it is granted us by God to find the tomb empty, what happens next?

A celebration, of course. That's why there is all that running and food in the Easter accounts: Peter and John running to the tomb, the Emmaus people running back to Jerusalem, food in the upper room when Jesus appears, fish on the seashore. It was a time for celebration.

And that is why churches which are always dark and somber and their people stuffy have somehow missed the point. Christians celebrate not because so many have daintily walked in the footsteps of Jesus, but because a stone has been rolled away. Celebration — the lifting up of the heart, praise, thanksgiving, and hand-clapping music — is natural to those who encounter an unexpected and ultimate victory over darkness and death.

But there is more. It's like a young boy or girl lost in a great city. Night comes with rain, and the child takes refuge under a bridge finally to be found there by flashlights held by parents who wrap the child in a coat and hold the child close. It's that child at home in the kitchen, being fed after a change into dry clothes, feeling safe and beginning to talk excitedly about adventures — about almost being hit by a car, locked doors, and people who would not listen. Then, a neighborhood kid knocks on the door. The rescued child stuffs a cookie in the pocket. "Where are you going?" "Out!" That's what salvation means. It means to be able to talk about where you've been in the darkness. It means hearing a knock on the door and going out again running, letting the screen door slam.

Easter is the joyful unexpectedness of rescue under a bridge on a dark and rainy night, being held close, going home, drying out, and going out again.

And that's why it's so strange that the church is the big American pussycat asleep by the hearth while fires smolder within the walls of the house. Why are those of us who believe in the resurrection still hunkered down before the warm glow of God's love?

Some are by the hearth because they really believe that the rescue under the bridge is the best part of the story. They believe that going home is what it's all about, the drying out and food and talk about how bad it was on the city streets. They are committed to being neat and tidy in the household of God.

But others of us hear a knock at the door — an invitation to come out and play, an invitation to sing some songs of empty tombs, gravestones rolled away, and of rescue under bridges. It's an invitation to come out and play.

Eventually, though, the one who knocks invites us on a journey which, if we will go, takes us into hospitals, hovels, and to distant lands. We are led on a journey which takes us past missiles in their silos and mountains of ammunition to the rooms where the aged sit silent or babbling amidst the memories of better years, and to prisons of many kinds. We are invited to hear stories of loneliness and shouts of anger, to participate in the pain of love and the work of justice.

Only the naive will fail to notice that we are headed up that hill toward crucifixion. It's dangerous to be involved in major conflicts and depressing to be involved with the victims of darkness. It's better to stay in the house.

Unless you've been to the tomb which lies beyond the hill of crucifixion and found it empty, it's better to stay at home. Stay inside unless at some time you've been met by the warm smile of a dark face on a nighttime city street and know it to be an experience of Good Friday's reversal by Easter.

And if salvation comes to mean more to you than just the warm embrace of rescue, then you will always hear a knock at the door and know it to be an invitation to come out again and to walk the cities' streets with him.

For those who live according to the flesh set their minds on the things of the flesh, but those who live according to the Spirit set their minds on the things of the Spirit. To set the mind on the flesh is death, but to set the mind on the Spirit is life and peace. For the mind that is set on the flesh is hostile to God; it does not submit to God's law, indeed it cannot; and those who are in the flesh cannot please God.

But you are not in the flesh, you are in the Spirit, if in fact the Spirit of God dwells in you. Any one who does not have the Spirit of Christ does not belong to him. But if Christ is in you, although your bodies are dead because of sin, your spirits are alive because of righteousness. If the Spirit of him who raised Jesus from the dead dwells in you, he who raised Christ Jesus from the dead will give life to your mortal bodies also through his Spirit which dwells in you.

Romans 8:5–11

9 | *Point and Counterpoint*

Not often, but sometimes, we get carried away. Years ago I visited a friend at his college. It was necessary for him to attend the tryouts for a musical that night, so I went along and sat in the back of the dark and empty theater. One by one the soloists stepped into the spotlight and sang a haunting melody which I can still hum, though the lyrics elude me. Why have I remembered that night for so long? It seemed as though the song was for me, and the best of the soloists took me to places I'd never been, showed me things I'd never seen, and allowed me to feel things I'd never felt before.

It happens to all of us. These are times, often mysterious, when the whole self grows. What our hearts and minds embrace is more than what had been embraced before. Romantic love has this capacity to evoke new and marvelous experiences. Or it may be our first sight of great mountains or the experience of childbirth. Sometimes it is a lecture which is different from any we've heard, not by content or form but by what is happening within us. The lecturer may know it too; that in the very act of speaking more has been embraced than was first intended.

Not often, but sometimes, the words of the Bible carry us away. They may be so familiar that it takes a special occasion for that to happen. Perhaps a visit to a country church when traveling alone and the sermon of a country preacher. We've heard it all before. But now we hear it differently, and listening to someone who hasn't given up and yielded to weariness makes us wonder about ourselves and our weariness and why we've given up.

Or consider from the back of the theater the people who fill the pages of the New Testament: Peter, James and John, Mary and Martha, Judas, of course. We've seen them up close most of our lives and perhaps played their roles in a pageant or two. But seen from a greater distance, from the back of a theater with the spotlight in between, it's possible to wonder about them. What makes them different? What makes them Christian?

The difference isn't really visible. Their clothing is ordinary. There is no Christian uniform, nothing special in their hands, on their heads — no pins, badges, collars, or halos. There is no common expression on all their faces. They speak with different accents, though leaning toward Galilean, which is not surprising. What makes them so special?

They are not more conservative than the general population. They go to the synogogue, as far as we know, but don't make a big thing out of it. They are generally unhappy about being occupied by the Romans, but they are not revolutionaries stockpiling weapons. Neither can they be described as bleeding hearts, as church people are sometimes described today. They brought people to Jesus for healing, but sometimes they were annoyed by those who came for healing and sent them away.

What makes them Christians and worthy of our remembrance?

They were not joggers. They ate whatever they could get: bread, fish, and wine, at least. Later on it's clear that they would eat anything, even meat which had been offered to idols, as long as such eating didn't give offense to someone else. In fact, they seemed to like potluck suppers, an element of discipleship which has persisted.

These people of the New Testament were aware of social class, but capable of crossing the lines, too. A fisherman like Peter seemed to get along fine with a bureaucrat like Matthew. They certainly leaned toward male chauvinism, but in that, too, they were part of their culture. In business they were a little careless and left their fishing and carpentry for long periods of time. They were often short of money, another characteristic which is found among their latter-day counterparts.

But what makes them Christians? It is "none of the above."

What makes them Christians is that they themselves had been transported by a song to see things which they had never seen before, to hear things they had never heard, and to feel things unfelt before. They came eventually to call themselves Christians because the voice which enlarged their embrace of life was the voice of Christ.

Like most of us, they had followed the rhythms of their blood; the rhythms of sleeping and waking, working and resting, feast and famine, begetting children and burying children, war and peace. They lived by the rhythm of the way things are, which is our rhythm too. A little greed and a little giving, loving and hating, and the laws which say when enough is enough. There once was a garden called Eden where things had been different, and there would be a Messiah sometime, but what was and will be hardly make a difference to the way things are. They hardly make a difference to those who live by the rhythms of blood.

What made these people different was that both the past and the future encountered them or the Messiah came to them or, in Saint Paul's language, they were possessed by the Spirit of Christ. How it's said isn't the important thing. What it meant to them was that they saw, felt, and heard things differently. There was a counterpoint to the rhythms of blood.

The point was that people of power are served by those with less power. The counterpoint is that the powerful are to be the servants of the weak.

The point was that the rich get richer. The counterpoint is that the rich are stewards of what they have and accountable to the human family for the use of their wealth.

The point was that sinners are stoned or shunned. The counterpoint is that sinners are embraced.

The point was that Galileans are nowhere and Samaritans nothing. The counterpoint is that a Galilean embodies the Word of God and Samaritans are teachers.

The point was that death was the end. The counterpoint is that death has lost its sting.

The point was that God had made promises to the descend-
ants of Abraham, Isaac, and Jacob. The counterpoint is
that the club is not that exclusive.

The litany is a long one. These people were Christians
because ringing in their ears was a counterpoint to the rhythms
of blood, to the melody of the way things are. That's what made
these people different.

Did the disciples live only out of their new understanding?
Are we now to be so holy that we are servants instead of people
of power being served? Are we the ones who share our riches,
embrace sinners, the ones who listen to Samaritans teach? Are
we the ones who have no fear of death and place the human
family everywhere above our particular nation or state?

Whether it should be so or not, it's hardly likely. We will
never in this life exchange point for counterpoint. Saint Paul
said rather that "if the Spirit dwells within you, then the God
who raised Christ will give new life to your mortal bodies," to
your rhythms of blood. In other words, we are not going to
leave the theater the same persons we were when we entered,
but we'll not be angels either. We have a drive for power, and
will have it, but now we have experienced the truth of servant-
hood too. And power for its own sake will never again go unchallenged within us.

Once we have known in our hearts the justice of stewardship
and of the rich being held accountable to God for their riches,
then the claim to do whatever we like with our resources will
never go unchallenged.

Once we've experienced ourselves as sinners embraced instead of shunned, then we will always be conflicted by our
shunning of other sinners and be challenged to embrace them.

A Christian is a person whose normal rhythms have been in-
terrupted by the counterpoint of heaven. We will not be angels,
but our lives will never again be as dull or as uncomplicated
either: not perfect, but not the same, and working for what is
better. We will be people who measure the meaning of life by
what we've now seen and heard and felt, just as the disciples

were not the same because the song of Christ had evoked within them new ways of envisioning life.

I attend a formal dinner and the man on my left, internationally respected as a man of finance, tells me that he is learning Hebrew and about Jewish ways of mourning, and that he daily reads the Psalms. The young man on my right, a business analyst, shares his search for a community of faith in Manhattan. The counterpoint of heaven is echoing in their ears. Here and there one person stops short another's telling of a racist story, while another wonders among her friends whether the tax reduction she will receive will hurt the poor. A young man hesitates before registering for the draft, anguished because he cannot be sure that peace can ever come through killing.

Not much else distinguishes Christians, nor should it any more than the first disciples could be distinguished by what they wore or ate, by their business acumen and learning, or lack of it. But there is something not easily seen which was at work in them, and is at work in many of us. It is hearing a song which evokes meanings new to us or long forgotten; a counterpoint to the rhythm of things as they are. It is being subject always to the disturbing and sometimes joyful echoing sound of Eden which names a future more humane than our present living. It is being subject to the rhythm of blood, but responding as well to the counterpoint of heaven. And somewhere along this journey of encounter and response some of us come to acknowledge that our lives are shaped by this equation and that, in ways more profound than ritual involvement, we are Christians.

"Woe to you, scribes and Pharisees, hypocrites! for you tithe mint and dill and cummin, and have neglected the weightier matters of the law, justice and mercy and faith; these you ought to have done, without neglecting the others. You blind guides, straining out a gnat and swallowing a camel!"

Matthew 23: 23-24

10 | Gnats and Camels

We can usually handle small sins: the occasional anger, saying "damn," getting drunk, a little gluttony here and there, a touch of envy, a bit of jealousy. These sins can cause grief, a lot of grief, but we can make good or absorb them. A kiss on the cheek, a smile, a handshake, and time; each is a household remedy for minor irritations. Not according to doctrine or in the sight of God or as theologians see it, but in the ordinary experience of ordinary people, small sins are an everyday occurrence which we've found ways of putting straight or putting behind us.

It's the other sins, the ones written large and corporate, the sins which neither smile nor handshake can touch, which deserve our major attention. The sins which time won't make go away, the camels we swallow while straining out gnats, these are the sins written in large type which are, nevertheless, hard for all but the prophets to read.

Ultimately, sin comes to its root in idolatry. Idolatry means that we have chosen one value or priority over another. It is a word which, in religious language, means to act in response to a value which we place above the will of God. Sometimes we make a conscious choice to respond to an alternate value and sometimes, as Saint Paul wrote, we seem to be drawn into such choices by forces beyond our control.

The gnats are everywhere. Policemen don't like to take drunks to the hospital because they might get sick in the patrol car, just as others of us reject hitchhikers in wet swimsuits. Our convenience dominates. And the more fastidious we are in our religious commitments, the more we strain out these gnats and

worry about our idolatry — placing a higher priority on the condition of our vehicle than on our commitment to acts of duty or
kindness.

Students with a commitment to God face these gnats every
day. Survival in a demanding academic climate competes with
the commitment to spend time with a lonely or troubled peer on
the floor below. Two priorities fight it out within us: a good
academic record and Christ's command to love our neighbors.
People of all ages wrestle with the command of God in Christ
not to lust, knowing full well the feelings of lust which rise in
spite of our good intentions. The more serious we are about our
desire to be faithful to God, the more troubled we are about the
ordinary sins, the reversal of values, which occur within us day
after day.

For the most part, though, this is small stuff compared with
those idolatries we practice as a part of society, the reversals of
values over which we seem to have so little control. We berate
ourselves because we don't pick up a hitchhiker in a wet bathing
suit but ignore our participation in a world economy in which
five hundred million people are undernourished or starving.
The total amount of food produced has increased, but so has the
number of people in the world, and the distribution of food is as
unequal as ever. It is not that all the world's people cannot be
adequately fed. They can be fed. We choose not to do that.
Why? Because one part of the world's people has the resources
to eat beef, and we have developed such a taste for it and for a
host of other foods that we have neither the will nor the desire
to change our eating habits in order to prevent the malnutrition
which robs other human beings of their potential and condemns
millions to death.

Why don't the various governments do something about this?
In plain language, it is because they are voting what they know
to be our desires. Their estimate is that we would prefer to live
as we do, even if that means that there is not enough food to go
around the world's table. That's sin written large.

Of course, church people are raising millions of dollars each
year to feed the hungry. Increasingly, this aid has been in terms

of specialists, equipment, and seed rather than sacks of grain—and that makes sense. It's obviously not a sin to give money to help the starving; it's benevolent, but probably a mistake. Nor is it stupid for the churches to raise money for this purpose because church leaders know that the people of the congregations would like to help. But it's probably a mistake because even a billion dollars a year would make only a beginning in solving the problem of world hunger. The money would be more effectively spent in educating ourselves to understand the high cost to others of our eating as we do and to appreciate what is happening to the soil and water supply as we attempt to get more and more from the limited arable land. The money would be more effectively spent in efforts to change our nation's priorities so that they reflect a long-term management of earth rather than short-term exploitation. The money would be more effectively spent in attempting to develop new international structures more likely to result in an equitable distribution of basic food supplies.

Most Christians know that our food consumption in the face of world hunger is offensive to God. We hesitate to own it as our sin because it seems removed from us and beyond our capacity to correct. World hunger is an institutionalized sin, and that makes it appear less personal, less like our own sin. But in a free society we cannot escape that easily. Our institutions are difficult to change, but they are subject to concerted effort by organized minorities which have a point of view and the will to pursue that view openly and intelligently. Our sin is compounded by our silence, or by the fact that we have allowed our church leaders and legislators to believe that we are content to give a few dollars a year to ameliorate the worst situations but have no desire for major changes.

What we have said is that our own well-filled table has a higher priority than the hungry people who are our brothers and sisters in Christ. That's idolatry. Christ didn't die on the cross because we use foul language. He died because we create institutions to do our sinning for us and will not put down our forks to change that.

We have known since 1974, and many knew before that time, that all the world's efficiently retrievable oil would be gone in the lifetime of most of us. Whether we found the remaining oil sooner or later made no difference in any essential way. There is a limited supply, and it cannot be replaced. It was three years until former President Carter declared the moral equivalent of war against this problem, and then he asked so little of us that it was difficult for people to believe that the problem was really serious.

We have no stomach for cutting down or cutting back. By 1981, it became clear that we would risk war to preserve our claim on Middle Eastern oil. Registration for the draft was reinstituted, and the new president cut billions of dollars from services to human beings and added it to the military budget. Mothballed ships were to be reactivated, new missile systems installed, and more advanced bombers were to be built. We would solve our energy problem without serious disruption of our consumptive life. Safety standards for nuclear power plants were relaxed, and more plants were to be built before we had solved the problem of nuclear waste disposal. More coal was to be burned, and regulations concerning air pollution were to be relaxed. In Boston, the weatherman began to announce not just how much it had rained but also the amount of acid in the rain and, consequently, in the streams, lakes, and soil.

Voices of protest have been heard, often within the churches. But the largest and most active of the churches concentrated on gnats, on the effort to make all abortions illegal, while the military buildup continued and the majority of the American people assumed that they could go on consuming the remaining supplies of oil simply because they had always lived that way and still had the money to buy it or, if need be, the muscle to fight for it. This is sin written large.

One of the most effective ways to force us to cut down our use of energy has been to hit us where we live: in the pocketbook. Institutions installed valves and computers to work the valves, and householders installed storm windows not to save oil for children and grandchildren or to make more oil available to developing nations, but because the cost of oil provoked efficiency. What this means, of course, is that those with the most money to invest in changing equipment save the most money. It also means that when gasoline becomes two dollars a gallon, some of us will still be able to drive our cars and vote against mass transportation when the poor have long since had to sell their cars and wonder how they are going to get to work on time. While all this was happening, Christians were busy trying to reinstitute prayer in the schoolroom.

The people of North America are only six percent of the world's population, but we consume about one-third of all the world's nonrenewable resources. It would be naive to assume that we would suddenly become virtuous and say, "Goodness, we are using more than our fair share of what's left. Let's change our style of life and share." It's not that easy, and we are not likely to become virtuous. But Christians, at least, should be honest enough to call this consumption what it is: sin — sin written large! It is institutionalized and therefore less personal, but still our sin. We make it clear every day by our silence and our demands that we idolize our consumptive life and give this style a higher priority than we give to God.

God is concerned about justice. When the last car, having burned the last drop of oil, rolls to a stop in the middle of the highway, God will plant a cross in the middle of the highway against its front bumper. All the world's poor will gather under that cross, and God will say quietly to us, "The weightier matters of the law, justice and mercy and faith; these you ought to have done, without neglecting the others. You blind guides, straining out a gnat and swallowing a camel!"

"Let not your hearts be troubled; believe in God, believe also in me. In my Father's house are many rooms; if it were not so, would I have told you that I go to prepare a place for you? And when I go and prepare a place for you, I will come again and will take you to myself, that where I am you may be also. And you know the way where I am going." Thomas said to him, "Lord, we do not know where you are going; how can we know the way?" Jesus said to him, "I am the way, and the truth, and the life; no one comes to the Father, but by me." . . . Philip said to him, "Lord, show us the Father, and we shall be satisfied."

John 14:1–6, 8

11 | *Heaven Must Wait*

There may be some people who stoically endure the present while they wait for a glorious life after death. Such waiting, after all, is a major theme in many a hymn, but it's hard to find many people who actually live as though life beyond death played much of a part in their present thinking.

Most of us are not embarrassed to be concerned about the present. From birth to at least mid-life we are in training for survival: learning how to secure food, speak, write, use tools, relate to others, rear children, and manage our affairs in a complex society. From mid-life to old age we work at accepting what we are or struggle to become something else. In old age we strive to live gracefully on less and hope that we die well. It is the ethical decisions and difficult choices of the present which demand attention. If God is to have a place in our lives, then it is this life and not some other in which we desire his compassion and aid.

Philip, one of Jesus' twelve disciples, would have understood this. He wasn't a very important person. He was important only in the sense in which every person makes a difference and in the sense that the world is impoverished by the loss of a single snowflake. But Philip was not particularly memorable, nor did he shape the course of the future. He is important to us because his approach was so modern. He saw the world as many of us see it and said some of the things which we might well have said if we had been there. Philip had little interest in the heaven to come and a genuine concern for life in its immediacy.

Though one of the twelve disciples, Philip appears in only three scenes in the Jesus story, which makes it easy to look quickly at all of the evidence.

In the first scene, he spoke to a man named Nathanael: "We have found him of whom Moses . . . wrote, Jesus of Nazareth." Nathanael, sharing the prejudices of his time, replied archly, "Can anything good come out of Nazareth?" Now it is Philip's answer to Nathanael's put-down which has a modern ring to it: "Nathanael, come and see!" He did not initiate a big discussion about the rise and fall of Nazareth or a philosophical debate about how good rises triumphant out of the ashes of a bad reputation. For Philip, verification is the issue: "Come and see." His response is direct, sensible, and cuts to the heart of the matter. We could have said it ourselves.

The second time we meet Philip is on that occasion when some five thousand people had gathered to hear Jesus. It was the time of Passover, when Jews remembered their deliverance from Egypt, the ancient time when they had gathered their belongings and fled from their oppressors. Jews had celebrated the Passover for millenia, but how were they going to celebrate in this place when there was no bread? Jesus asked the question of Philip, perhaps because it was precisely Philip's kind of question: "How are we to buy bread so that these people may eat?" So Philip, with the eye of an accountant and the head of a purchasing agent, looked around. It couldn't be done. "Two hundred denarii would not buy enough bread for each of them to get a little," he reported. He was correct: not enough money and no baker likely to have that quantity of bread even if they had the money.

It never occurred to Philip, being prototype of ourselves, that the bread would be provided miraculously. Even though it was the time of miracles — the celebration of the passing over of the angel of death, the parting of the Red Sea, and bread provided in the wilderness. Pious people might have made the connection and anticipated a miracle, but it didn't occur to Philip. It probably would not have come to our minds either. Facts are what count, and the fact was that there wasn't enough money to buy bread and no baker capable of providing it.

Philip appears a third time in the last days of Jesus' life. Jesus had just washed the disciples' feet, the Last Supper had been eaten, and the betrayal of Judas had been announced. Jesus then tried once more to help his disciples understand what God was doing among them and how his coming death was in some way the beginning of a new creation.

Thomas had already asked his question: "Lord, . . . how can we know the way?" Jesus had replied, "I am the way." Then a word from our man Philip: "Lord, show us the Father, and we shall be satisfied."

Consider the progression. At the beginning, Philip had seen enough of God at work in Jesus that he invited Nathanael to come and see it too. But whatever confidence he had that Jesus was the Messiah did not overcome his accountant's approach to the bread problem. He expected no miracle. Finally, when the chips were down and Jesus said, "I am the way," Philip responded with what most of us eventually say: "Show us the Father."

Philip had seen people healed and fed, and good news preached. "Have you been with me so long, and yet do not know me, Philip? He who has seen me has seen the Father. . . ." But to Philip and to many of us, such seeing is ambiguous. It is not the kind of seeing to which we can bring others who, by the self-authenticating nature of what they see, must automatically agree that we have now, together, seen the Father. So having seen Jesus, heard Jesus, witnessed his life and miracles, and heard him say that whoever has seen him has seen the Father, Philip simply repeats his request: "Show us the Father, and we shall be satisfied."

And that is something which will not happen. Even Moses was refused his request to see the glory of God not because God plays games with us, but because once we've seen the glory of God there is no way we can say no to God. If we cannot say no to God, our yes means nothing.

God comes hidden. He came hidden even in Jesus, the one in whom God chose to reveal himself. It was possible for Peter to deny him, which is why Peter's confession of faith becomes the rock on which the church is built. It was possible for Judas to betray Jesus. It was possible for Philip to hear Jesus say, "I am the way," and to respond, "Show us the Father, and we shall be satisfied." Philip was a modern person, asking for the kind of verification we have been taught to expect. It is hard for modern types to accept the hiddenness of God and even harder to understand that God's refusal is a gift, the only condition within which the words "faith," "trust," and "love" make any sense.

The reasons for this aren't important here. What is important is the biblical witness and its echoes in our own experience. God comes hidden; he comes most fully but also hidden in Jesus of Nazareth. And Philip, our spiritual brother, wants more, and will be given no more, just as we are given neither more nor less than God hidden and revealed in Jesus of Nazareth.

The time and place of meeting is always our present. In the midst of our learning to speak, we hear God-language. In the midst of our attempt to provide security for ourselves, there is a witness concerning what makes us secure. As we experience our sexuality, there is a witness about God's intentions for our sexuality. It is highly unlikely that in anything approaching a literal sense we will meet Jesus or God in the way in which modern people like Philip would prefer it. What we do encounter are options, choices, and a variety of ways of understanding and defining ourselves — our purposes and goals. What we encounter are varieties of ways in which worth and value are measured, one of which bears the imprint of Christ.

Whatever knowledge of God we may receive in life beyond death, hopefully a vision of the glory of a compassionate Creator, what we get now is a word spoken about God. It may be abstract words — words about God's love, the strength God gives, or the forgiveness which he offers — but abstractions seldom make much difference in our lives. The helpful word about God is much more specific. It is addressed to our sense of failure in a particular competition. It is spoken to us as we look in the mirror and judge ourselves attractive or unattractive. It is spoken at the moment we curl our lip in a sneer, the moment our child takes our hand, or when we are moved sideways rather than upward in the company for which we work. The Word of God which is helpful is the one which comes to our ears and hearts when the drums begin to roll, when the street-walker smiles, when we hear the announcement that we are to be honored or are about to die.

The word we hear may be ambiguous: a phrase from a hymn, a remembered verse of the Bible, a pull somewhere deep within us which could be anything from the prejudice of a grand-mother to the prompting of Almighty God. God is so hidden, the whisperings of angels and demons so intermingled, that it's perhaps safest to write it off altogether and follow the logic of self-interest.

There is another way to go, however, the first step of which is to clarify for ourselves the difference between a grandmother's prejudice and the Word of God, the difference between the message of angels and the speech of demons. There are, after all, ways of finding out at least the basic outlines of what Jews and Christians have said about their experience of God. There is a consistent theme running through the scriptures and the teachings of Jews and Christians which even those with limited intelligence and training can comprehend. What excuse is there for not learning it?

The second step is to take some risks. It is highly unlikely, in spite of what might be preached in our churches, that we will encounter the hidden God in our present unless we risk doing the things which God requires of us in those situations in which obedience is tested. What is the word of the Lord to us when a nation prepares for war? What is the word of the Lord to us when we see an unattractive or an attractive face in the mirror? What does that word require of us, and will we risk the doing of it?

A large number of young people approaching draft age are wondering about whether they are conscientious objectors. How do they know whether the quiet voice within them is the word of the Lord, fear, or a simple unwillingness to interrupt their lives with military training? The only way to sort it out is to risk attempting the life of nonviolence. It means facing those times which come every day when we have the choice of raising the ante or of stepping back. It is the risk of choosing to de-escalate. There may be other ways of encountering God in our present, but the only one which most of us know is to pay attention to the Christian witness in a concrete moment of choice and to risk obedience. It's these moments of choice which inform our prayers and which our prayers empower us to face.

Many of us are throwing away the blessings of family life to meet the demands of our job. One voice says we have to work as we do, but the witness which grows out of the church's experience of God is that the family must come first. The risk that's required is to get our job restructured, or to look for another one. More easily said than done? Of course. But if we refuse to take that risk, then we've yielded not only our family life but a major opportunity to encounter the God who is hidden in the world of our present and its times of decision.

Every time we decide whether or not to visit an elderly person, to contribute food, to ruin or salvage another person's life, to lie or to tell the truth, to drink or not when driving, to cut down or not on consumption of food and nonrenewable resources, to use our vote for the self or the common good – at each of these points of decision there is an opportunity to take the risk of responding to what we understand to be the Christian way of doing life. We may well wish that God or Jesus were standing there in plain sight giving us an unambiguous signal and cheering us on. That's not likely. First we take the risk, according to the best understanding we've allowed ourselves to obtain. It is then, in the midst of the risk-taking, that many of us have come closest to meeting the God who is otherwise hidden in human history.

If there is any threat to us in the life beyond death, it is probably the judgment which falls upon those who fail to take the risks of obedience by which faith comes to maturity.

Like Philip, we are modern people. Seeing is believing and miracles seldom occur to us. "Show us the Father, and we shall be satisfied." But, for our sake, God comes hidden, and there will be no seeing of the glory of God for those who will not risk. The miracles of God will always be miracles which happen to someone else and the meaning of faith will always be a meaning belonging to someone else until we have understood that the ways of God and the ways of the world around us are in conflict, and that the experience of God's embrace belongs to those with the courage to choose, even when the choices are themselves ambiguous.

Philip was not wrong in desiring assurance. He was wrong only in desiring it before he acted, rather than offering that obedience within which assurance is given.

"You have heard that it was said, 'An eye for an eye and a tooth for a tooth.' But I say to you, Do not resist one who is evil. But if any one strikes you on the right cheek, turn to him the other also; and if any one would sue you and take your coat, let him have your cloak as well; and if any one forces you to go one mile, go with him two miles. Give to him who begs from you, and do not refuse him who would borrow from you.

"You have heard that it was said, 'You shall love your neighbor and hate your enemy.' But I say to you, Love your enemies and pray for those who persecute you, so that you may be sons (children) of your Father, who is in heaven; for he makes his sun rise on the evil and on the good, and sends rain on the just and on the unjust. For if you love those who love you, what reward have you? Do not even the tax collectors do the same? And if you salute only your brethren, what more are you doing than others? Do not even the Gentiles do the same? You, therefore, must be perfect, as your heavenly Father is perfect."

Matthew 5:38–48

12 | *Exclusive or Inclusive*

"You . . . must be perfect!"

Few imperatives have caused so much grief and hatred in the human family. Parents who by word, example, or unspoken expectation lay this burden upon their children, prepare the foundation for their children's self-denying grief or overweening self-esteem. They lay the groundwork for the anger which, fueled by a demand which can't be met, is turned against those who laid it down.

But perfection is beautiful, and that should be acknowledged first. Walk around Zion and behold. There was an old and imperfect way. The old way was a broken tooth for a broken tooth. That was fair enough, but not perfect. Perfection is the silence of a blow unreturned and the cycle of violence ended. There was a way by which a judge decided what was right. Perfection is the silence of two contestants who have agreed along the way. Perfection is a coat taken off and given to those in need. Perfection is peacemaking and serenity of spirit.

"You . . . must be perfect!" Before you feel the judgment of it, appreciate its beauty. Perfect is a garden where night's dew sparkles in the morning sun. It is the silent touch of love's embrace, a multicolored fabric spun of holiness.

Before perfection judges our imperfection, it names what is true. Truth, as religious people define it, is that perfection which God intends. What is most fully true is that love which salutes not only neighbors and friends, but the love which embraces the enemy. Not because this is a good idea or honors an ideal, but because it is the perfection of love as God defines love and as he requires that we practice it.

Does it make any difference what God desires or how he defines perfection? Isn't our conduct really a matter of social contract in which we essentially say to one another, "If you let me alone, I'll stay away from you?" G. K. Chesterton was one of many who believed that the control of our behavior is not that rational. First, said Chesterton, we agree that we should not do certain things in the holy place. Our behavior is first a response of awe and restraint in the presence of the Perfect, of Truth. The limitation of the social contract is that the strong need have no fear of the weak, and the weak are therefore victims of the strong; no contract can protect them. But even the strong become cautious in the presence of the Holy One, especially when God is believed to be the defender of the weak.

To whatever extent this is true, all of us who know the danger of the imperative, "You . . . must be perfect," are well advised to respect it. If there is no holy place where human beings take off their shoes and bow in reverence, then the strong will define truth and the weak will die or lick boots. The social contract is small comfort unless it is undergirded by a Truth to which all give at least deference. There can be no holiday from violence and duress unless holiness is named and honored.

It is also important to say that this is not the gospel of Jesus Christ. Reverence for the God who names the perfect and bids us do it, is a foundation on which all human societies depend. But it is not the gospel because when the perfect is named, our imperfection, our sin, is also named. To be in the presence of the Holy One is to know our unholiness. We have two options. We either live always with a sense of guilt and failure, or we can lie to ourselves. There is no good news in either response.

Luther once said that the last bastion of sin is morality. The assumption that we are moral people or that we can be perfect is the illusion to which we cling the longest. It is the asumption that we can obey the Ten Commandments or that we can love with the perfection which turns the other cheek — that we are truly generous, that we are capable of doing the truth and of walking with satisfaction in the holy place. When we place God's command, "You . . . must be perfect," on one side and our attempts to respond on the other side and delare it a balanced equation, we are sectarians and not Christians, dangerous to ourselves and to the commonwealth. This is the kind of pride which presumes to legislate one's own view of morality for the obedience of the whole population.

The good news, the gospel of the New Testament, does not lie in the command to be perfect and beautiful, however necessary that command is. The good news is that God is compassionate toward those who dare to look perfection in the face and to acknowledge that they are not worthy to stand in the holy place. The gospel is that Jesus died for the redemption of the whole world. It speaks inclusive language because there are no uncompromised people. Every human being shares guilt for the undernourishment of a billion neighbors, for Hiroshima and the Holocaust. Every human being is obviously capable of love, but who would deny that that love is often lust or that we, by reflection upon our own goodness, shatter our newly placed halo. The good news is not "You . . . must be perfect." The good news is that God is merciful toward the compromised, the rattlers of teeth, and the clutchers of coats. The scandal of Christianity is not that perfection is required, but that God suffers to embrace the imperfect.

Our country is enduring a major conflict over the issue of abortion. All who honor God, and others as well, know what perfect is. Perfection is two parents who love and honor one another and are faithful to one another. It is these two parents who in love and desire bring forth a child, a healthy child, who rejoices the hearts of his or her parents. It is that child surrounded by affection and wise teaching who grows into adulthood and becomes capable of being both responsible and loving.

We know what perfection is, and most of the people known to us desire it for themselves and for their children. Anyone who says that those women who now seek abortion are ignorant of the ideal or that they take abortions lightly are reflecting their prejudice and not a knowledge of these women. They haven't met the teenager deceived by an older man, the older woman who knows through amniocentesis that her unborn child is defective, or the woman never strong enough to establish control over her own body. All of these people know what perfection is and they know that abortion is wrong, that it is not the fullness and holiness which God desires. But the perfection which God desires is not one of their alternatives. They choose not between brilliant light and dark shadow, but between two evils. All they ask of us, and pray God might grant them, is the strength to make the best decision which they can make, and the compassion and mercy which will hold them in their suffering. Throw the first stone if you like, but I believe that when we do, it is more often Jesus Christ that we strike because he is kneeling there at that woman's side. The last bastion of sin is that assumed morality which would in the name of God legislate away that woman's right to endure the agony of a decision which is hers to make before her Maker. Our task is to hold such people close, as God most certainly does.

Some people rail at Saint Paul for complicating the simple teachings of Jesus given in the Sermon on the Mount. Others of us bless Saint Paul every day because he tells us of Christ crucified for the salvation of those who are judged and condemned by the simple teachings of Jesus. He wrote to the Romans, "If it is possible, so far as it depends upon you, live peaceably with all." Why didn't he just say, "Be perfect and live peaceably with all." It was because he knew that the whole creation groans in travail, that perfection is not possible, that it doesn't all depend upon us, that human genes are defective sometimes, and that human beings are aggressive in their sin. He said, "if it be possible" and "so far as it depends upon you" because salvation does not depend upon our perfection, but upon the compassion of God who in Christ suffered for the compromised.

Most of us have an enormous distaste for controversy but I, at least, am driven to make distinctions concerning the way in which the gospel is preached and understood. The obligation to make such distinctions falls upon both the preacher and those who listen from the pew. However weak and ineffective we think the church may be, it is nevertheless painfully clear that much of what is happening in our national life has its roots in the misrepresentation of the gospel that emanates from too many pulpits.

We can use either inclusive language or exclusive language. We can say, as Jesus did, that God sends the gentle rain upon the just and the unjust alike and, as Saint Paul did, that Christ died for all, that all of us sin and fall short of the glory of God, that the whole world groans, that the last bastion of sin is morality, that we love God only because he first loved us, that his compassion is unbounded, and that his Spirit fills the whole world. We can use the inclusive language of the Bible.

On the other hand, we can choose to use exclusive language, as do many of our preachers. We can talk about having chosen Jesus, and this sets us over and against those who have not chosen him. We can talk about our regeneration over and against those not reborn. We can preach about our sanctification over and against those who are not improving their moral behavior. We can preach only about personal sins, the lust in our hearts, our unlovely thoughts, our failures in generosity, and exclude from our thought altogether the way in which our sin is written into laws and built into corporate structures. We can exclude from consideration all the ways in which the world is broken, from defective genes to the rape of the land's fertility.

The consequences of exclusive language are devastating. It is "we" and "they" language: those who have chosen God standing apart from those who have failed to heed his call. It is those of us who are "moral" writing laws to coerce the "immoral." It is the sanctified seeking to impose upon others the sanctification which we presume to have attained. It is seeing poverty and crime primarily as the result of faulty moral choices and excluding those who make such choices not only from our embrace, but also from the embrace of God. It is speaking haughtily about tolerating or accepting the sinner, these lesser persons who had better shape up if they are to breathe the air of this great nation with its manifest destiny to spread the holiness which we assume to be our normal practice.

All of this is a far cry from Saint Paul when he writes, "If it is possible, as much as lies in you. . . ." This is a far cry from the Jesus who did not merely tolerate or accept sinners, but received them and ate with them. Exclusive language is not good news for those who are compromised, and who know that to be a fact about themselves which no pious talk will change.

If exclusive language results in these kinds of attitudes on the part of the political and religious right, it is equally disastrous when it comes from the big mouths of those on the liberal left as they attack the right. Increasingly, the poor and the oppressed are not received by liberals as loved by God or as brothers and sisters in compromise, but are manipulated and exploited as means to be used in the march toward personal power. It makes for sharp images and easily mined laughter when so-called liberals imply that all industrialists are evil, all labor leaders are criminals, all media evangelists are merely gathering money, and that all those who support increased military budgets are killers of babies. Once all of these people have been thus named, they can obviously be rejected as those outside the limits of decency — legitimate targets. It is so easy to exclude, especially if it can be done in the name of morality and justice and if we can make our exclusion, not one at a time, but by category.

Jesus was, of course, not wrong when he called us to perfection. Neither are parents wrong when they lay before their children that perfection which is the love and holiness of God. To teach and preach perfection is disastrous only when we equate it with the gospel. Not only children, but all of us should know what perfect is: that it is silence replacing the sound of broken teeth and the breaking of the cycle of violence. We are indeed called to make peace on the way to court, to take off our shoes in the holy place so that humankind may have a holiday from murder. But all of the perfection which we behold in God and teach our children will come only as judgment, and will be turned into anger unless we also hear our Lord say that the compassion of God falls like the gentle rain upon both the just and the unjust — that God spreads a table in the midst of shadowed valleys, provides a wedding garment for those whose righteousness is rags, and turns our bitter grapes into good wine. It is out of our forgiveness by a merciful God that we will find the humility to acknowledge those sins which we share with the whole human family and the strength to attempt once again those things which are good, acceptable, and perfect.

"It was also said, 'Whoever divorces his wife, let him give her a certificate of divorce.' But I say to you that every one who divorces his wife, except on the ground of unchastity, makes her an adulteress; and whoever marries a divorced woman commits adultery."

Matthew 5:31–32

"Come, let us return to the Lord;
   for he has torn, that he may heal us;
   he has stricken, and he will bind us up.
After two days he will revive us;
   on the third day he will raise us up,
   that we may live before him.
Let us know, let us press on to know the Lord;
   his going forth is sure as the dawn;
   he will come to us as the showers,
   as the spring rains that water the earth."

Hosea 6:1–3

13 | A Loved Face

The setting for Albert Camus's *The Plague* is a city in North Africa which has been cut off from the world by an outbreak of the plague. Hundreds die each day, and among the living all joy has long since departed. One of the characters looks into a shop window at Christmas, remembering his wife's face and knowing that he may never see her again. Camus provides this reflection by a doctor who witnesses the scene: "[The Doctor] knew what the old man was thinking as his tears flowed and thought it, too; that a loveless world is a dead world, and always there comes an hour when one is weary of prisons, of one's work and devotion to duty, and all one craves for is a loved face, the warmth and wonder of a loving heart." (Quoted in Robert Luccock, *If God Be for Us* [New York: Harper and Brothers, 1954], p. 81.)

Whatever foolish or trivial things we may say at a wedding, it is the longing of the old man which is the meaning of the wedding day. We all live in plague-struck cities, in prisons of various kinds. Our days are filled with work and devotion to duty. There comes a time, more frequent than many of us admit, when we can hardly bear another day of it, another hour; a time when we long only for a loved face, the warmth and wonder of a loving heart. The bride and groom each affirm that the other is the object of such a longing; they desire that it should always be so, and make their vow.

What they may or may not understand is the great danger of such love. To give oneself so wholly to another is to entertain not only the satisfaction of our deepest longing, but to risk the constant shaking of that which has become central to our security. The words of the marriage service, "for better for worse, for richer for poorer, in sickness and in health," receive their meaning only when we experience what worse, sickness, and poverty can mean. It's not just that one suffers from the short-comings of the other. Love's largest torment is the discovery of limitations within oneself, how small are the gifts we have to give to the one whose embrace is the largest meaning of our life. The silence of the other has its torment only because we love; anger strikes so deeply only because we love; separation is pain-ful because this other is to us the warmth and wonder of a lov-ing heart.

What bride and groom pledge to one another they cannot keep. There will be times of insensitivity to the pain and lostness of the other which are far worse than a blow; infidelities of various kinds, known and unknown. Nevertheless, they vow to live beyond their capacity, to set themselves against the odds. To whatever extent they fall short, it is falling short of the most glorious truth we know. Painful as such a shortfall is, we prefer it to the cynicism of making some lesser vow.

If the shortfall is so great that instead of craving the other's face we fear it, then what? If all the loveliness of eyes beholding is gone, and our life is seared by life together, then divorce.

Of course Jesus said no to divorce! So does the church. Why would that seem strange? Those who have been through it still cry in pain and are not hesitant to warn us. The increasing number of divorces does not mean that people have changed their minds and now affirm divorce, nor that we have searched the scriptures and suddenly discovered that Jesus favored divorce. That's nonsense. No one says that divorce is good, even when it is the choice which must be made.

What the church has done, and with some obvious scriptural support, is to emphasize the importance of monogamous mar-riage, the holiness of marriage, by strictures against divorce. the result is that the full weight of the church affirms those who have stayed married, regardless of the quality of the marriage, and condemns those who seek divorce.

We need the support of the religious community, carrot and

stick. Nevertheless, there are circumstances when love dies and the marriage is not only a hollow shell, but life destroying. A marriage can become so tortured that not only do we die within it, but our children also die. Knowing that a marriage takes effort, we have tried. Knowing that we sometimes need help, we have sought professional counseling and often prayed. Knowing that rebuilding takes time, we have tried time and again to rebuild. Knowing that divorce is so painful and destructive, we have been driven to do whatever can be done. Not perfectly and completely, because we are neither perfect nor complete people, but we have tried. Then, when all has failed and the death and dying within marriage continues, let us, invoking the mercy of God, proceed to divorce. No one needs to tell us that we have failed, sinned, violated the desire of God. The divorcing person with any remembrance of holy things knows that better than any who would pronounce such a judgment.

The question is not whether the divorced person has been adequately admonished or penalized. The question is whether there is any mercy, or whether the divorced person must forever wear a scarlet "D" upon the forehead and forever be refused a new beginning.

No one who has entered into the life of Jesus can put limits on the radical mercy of God, or believe that he is not present in our own weeping, or doubt that he reaches to embrace his children tormented by the anguish of a loved face lost.

We were fools, those of us who in our intellectual snobbery rejected the church's teaching that all are sinners and fall short of the glory of God. It is taught not only because it is true, but to keep us humble and remind us about kettles and pots both scorched by the fire. When we no longer think of ourselves as sinners, it is easier to throw stones at those whose sins become public.

The time for repentance has come. The kingdom of God is at hand, not demanding the repentance of those divorced. That has already occurred and will continue to be part of their prayers. Now it is the time of repentance for those who insist that there is one offense which neither God nor God's children can ever forgive. There is a new beginning for the man who kills, if with broken and contrite heart such a man desires it. There is a new beginning for imperfect parents who repent, thieves who repent. There is a new beginning for those who divorce. What God has given, let none of us take away.

Whether we rejoice to be given a single beginning in marriage or to begin marriage a second time, it helps to use a little common sense. In what we now call the traditional marriage of earlier generations, the man was freed to compete. This wasn't as true for those who worked a fixed number of hours and were locked into a particular kind of work. But in whole classes of the population, particularly the educated, the husband was freed to be a "go-getter," as the older generation put it. The husband was freed to work as long as he liked or felt he must — to travel, come home tired, put on his slippers, and fall asleep until the next day's competition began. The wife, of course, was the one who freed the husband to enjoy this sport, which was never called sport but "working his fingers to the bone." But it was sport, and trophies were given in the form of wage increases, bonuses, and a bigger desk. The military was very open about all of this and provided pins which could be worn to show one's rank. Academics were also given rank and robes to match. The wife made this sport possible because she ran the home and saw to it that the children were reared, the clothes washed, the beds made, and food put on the table. Sometimes the wife was given status based on the number of children she was able to bear and manage, but more often her status depended upon how well her husband played the game.

Now we have come to a modern time, and both wives and husbands are encouraged to enjoy the competition. It seems that we are as locked in as we were before, because there isn't much choice. Both wife and husband feel that they must work long hours because that's the way the game is played. Especially when we are new to a position, it is important to pay attention, travel when it serves the company, publish when the time is right and go where the opportunities are the greatest.

And now it is time for common sense. In the traditional marriage, the wife paid the highest personal cost. In modern marriage, when both husband and wife shoot for the top, it is wife and husband and children who suffer. There can be no lasting marriage to which time is not given. The quick answer is always, "We're giving one another quality time, which is better than quantity." That's nonsense. What kind of quality can there be when both husband and wife return to a dark house beat up by their respective days on the job, and there are still the routine household duties to be done? What time is there for the preparation of the celebrations about the table, for the building of the family saga, the play and adventure by which a loved face grows more lovely? One of the more tragic things occurring in our time is the early planting of these bitter seeds within the home.

In plague-struck cities, people like ourselves will often look into Christmas windows and know that a loveless world is a dead world, that one's work and devotion to duty is not enough, and that we crave the warmth and wonder of a loving heart. Christian men who have come to understand and repent the imbalance of relationships in the traditional marriage will know that we have no right to urge a return to it. Christian women have no desire for its return. The issue for us is the rejection of our previous subservience to the demands of the marketplace. The issue is whether we will have the personal strength and the support of the church to limit the investment of our time and energy on the job in order to have time and energy for one another and for our children. Given the culture, this could well mean fewer promotions, less money, and a smaller desk. We will probably set no track records, and in a culture which gives status to winners, this will be exceedingly difficult. But then, the Christian way of ordering priorities has always been in conflict with the way things are more generally done. And given the outcome of doing things the normal way, there's much to be said for a change.

And when the seventh month had come, the children of Israel were in their towns. And all the people gathered as one man into the square before the Water Gate; and they told Ezra the scribe to bring the book of the law of Moses which the Lord had given to Israel. . . . And Ezra opened the book in the sight of all the people, for he was above all the people; and when he opened it all the people stood. And Ezra blessed the Lord, the great God; and all the people answered, "Amen, Amen," lifting up their hands; and they bowed their heads and worshiped the Lord with their faces to the ground.

Nehemiah 8:1–3, 5–6

14 | *War Is Not Inevitable*

What is so insidious about seemingly harmless movies like "Star Wars" and "The Empire Strikes Back" is that they perpetuate the fantasy that warfare can continue in the future as it has in the past. Scientists warn that the level of radiation from the sun will increase to lethal proportions if we don't stop using pressurized cans for shaving soap and dessert topping. How can anyone believe that the radiation from nuclear warfare will mean anything other than the destruction of human life as we know it? Moreover, it is impossible for those of us who lived through the Holocaust and the atomic bombing of Japan to believe that nuclear weapons will never be used. Civilization as we know it hangs now by the slenderest of threads.

Christians have always believed that warfare is contrary to the will of God and that we are called to be peacemakers. Some Christians have been thoroughly consistent and have refused to become members of armed forces. Some have agreed to induction, but have refused to bear arms. The largest number of Christians, however, have lived by the "just war" ethic. Assuming that they live in a broken world, they have agreed to bear arms when they were convinced that a given war itself was less evil than the evil which that war sought to end. For example, it was assumed by many of us that the evils of the Third Reich were greater than the human cost of the Second World War. Christians never call war good or anything other than evil, but we assume that it could be the lesser of two evils and the most acceptable decision.

Christians can no longer support such a position. Nuclear war can never be the lesser evil. We have also arrived at a time in human history when there are alternatives to war for containing aggression. The time has come to shift our energies from military solutions to the development of effective regional and global structures which are furnished with economic, political, judicial, and police powers sufficiently strong to contain the ethnocentrism of nation states.

There are reasons to scoff at the notion that the Christian church will take leadership in the effort to abandon war as the ultimate means of resolving differences. There is a sense, however, in which what is likely makes no difference. Christians are called to do the will of God, or at least to say publicly what they believe the will of God to be, and to trust God to make something of their witness. Moreover, there is historical evidence, the Reformation for example, that the church can respond both to new truth and to a call to renewed faithfulness.

Four hundred years before the birth of Christ, the Jews were released from captivity in Babylon and returned to Jerusalem to rebuild the temple and the city walls. What was more important was the task of rebuilding their identity as a people, the restoration of the law, the will of God, as the cornerstone of their self-understanding.

Ezra the priest gathered the whole of the people in the city square, nearly fifty thousand, including 245 singers! A wooden pulpit had been built, the book of the law was laid on it, and when the book was opened, all the people stood. Silence fell, and for three hours Ezra read the law of Moses. The Levites helped the people to understand; they gave the sense of it. Ezra blessed the Lord, the great God, and all the people answered, "Amen! Amen!" They bowed and worshiped the Lord with their faces to the ground.

Out beyond the walls of Jerusalem was another world, other cultures, other ways of understanding what it means to be human beings. But what did it mean to be a Jew? It meant to worship one God, not many—a God who was still active with promises to keep. It was all in the book from which Ezra read: texts about giving thanks and being faithful, about a great time to come for those who keep faith, about peace and justice, honesty and honor, and not coveting or murdering. It was all in the book, and the people were attentive. They bowed their heads saying, "Amen!"

It wasn't that the Jews would always keep this law. They would let its spirit harden like ice, as we do. But they knew who they were. They were the people of the law, honored in the breach as well as in its keeping. That was their calling, and they have fulfilled that calling into our own time. Ezra opened the book, and all the people stood.

Four hundred years after Ezra read, there was a similar though smaller scene in the town of Nazareth. Jesus went into the synagogue. The attendant gave him the book of the prophet Isaiah, and the people stood attentive as he read, "The Spirit of the Lord is upon me, because he has anointed me to preach good news to the poor. . . . to proclaim release to the captives and recovering of sight to the blind, to set at liberty those who are oppressed, to proclaim the acceptable year of the Lord." He closed the book and gave it to the attendant. The people waited. He said, "Today this scripture has been fulfilled in your hearing."

To be a Christian means to define oneself, the purpose, joys, and responsibilities of one's life, after the image of truth which God has provided in Jesus of Nazareth. It is to believe that the largest truth about the self's humanity is that we are brothers and sisters to every other person on earth; that all these others are our neighbors, and that we are called to cherish and serve them. It is to believe that whatever evil has drawn or driven us to war, enslavement, or denigration, God has overcome that evil and desires to overcome it in us. It is to trust that the kingdom which has come in Christ will have its fullness, and that we are to be the people in the world who hold that hope against the darkness.

What is all of this opening of the book and reading? It is the drama within which both Jews and Christians rehearse their identity. We are Americans, many of us, but we are first and foremost people who serve one God, the God of Abraham, Isaac, and Jacob—the God disclosed with fullness in Jesus

Christ. We are defined by our response to the command of God and by our hope in the promise of God. We are not fools. We know that we live in a world of pain and cruelty. What we profess is not always possible. Nevertheless, it is our calling to say that the God we serve wills peace. It is our calling not to clap and throw our hats in the air when registration for the draft is announced, when a bill for armaments passes the Congress, when another nation is shown a line and told that if they cross it, they will be bombed to dust. These things are not clapping matters for Christians and Jews. It is a time for hanging black paraments upon our altars and for penitential prayers.

To be hearers of the Word means that we cannot join others who assume that the oil of the Middle East belongs simply to us because we have become accustomed to consuming it, or because we have the money to purchase it and the power to keep it from others. We are peculiar people, believing that the earth's resources belong ultimately to God and that we are called to share them not only with others now on earth, but to conserve them also for future generations. We are the people who are a little crazy in the matter of turning out the lights, driving less, and living more simply—not primarily for economic reasons (though that too), but because overconsumption is a cause of war, and we are called to be the makers of peace.

Christians aren't born without appetites. If it has a name, some of us desire it, covet it, and hoard it. But we know another truth and are called to practice that truth. Beyond the minimal requirements for food, shelter, and the freedoms which make for human dignity, there is little correlation between what we possess and our happiness. We may desire many things, but what we most deeply long for is to be loved and to love, to be at peace with one another, to give ourselves to useful work, and to rejoice in play and song.

Who would deny that good things come of war, too? War can unite a nation, as it did in the Second World War. Within many of us there are fantasies of uniforms and the camaraderie of the service, of ribbons which name the shadows we have endured and the far places we have seen. Christians are not immune to these fantasies. We are called to keep them under control.

Everywhere in our land some persons experience a growing fear of the devastation of nuclear war. How does all this reading from the book address these fears? It tells us that what is to be feared is not our own deaths. That is coming anyway, though later is preferred to sooner. The ultimate fear is that of not being true to what we believe is the meaning of our lives and central to our calling. It is the fear of being carried along with the crowd—with the slogans, assumptions, and cynicism that increasingly dominate our news and common conversations. It is the fear of standing for nothing important when it's clear that there are alternatives to war which demand our support. Disloyalty to one's country is a serious matter, but the ultimate fear for Christians and Jews is the fear of disloyalty to the promise of God, to the vision of a more graceful and compassionate life. The greatest fear is that we will bless evil with the name of God and deny the inheritance which he has promised.

In these days when thoughtful people everywhere proclaim the terrible danger of nuclear war, no one needs to defend a clear stand against military adventures or to defend a demand for nuclear disarmament. If there is anyone who needs to explain, it is those who would lead us closer to the abyss. And let's hear no more among us about a lack of patriotism. To love one's country in these days can only mean a clear no to those who would define strength in military terms. Such a definition will be the death of us all.

Sometimes when the book is opened and the reading defines who we are as Jews and Christians, the consequence is impractical. This makes no difference because it is still the truth as we understand it, and truth requires a hearing whether it is practical or not. But we have come to a time in human history when what is read from the book is both true and practical. Now is the time for Jews and Christians both to name and to practice the truth as both the Torah and Christ define it. The ultimate disloyalty to God and country is to believe that war is inevitable.

"These things I have spoken to you, while I am still with you. But the Counselor, the Holy Spirit, whom the Father will send in my name, he will teach you all things, and bring to your remembrance all that I have said to you. Peace I leave with you; my peace I give to you; not as the world gives do I give to you. Let not your hearts be troubled, neither let them be afraid. You heard me say to you, 'I go away, and I will come to you.' If you loved me, you would have rejoiced, because I go to the Father; for the Father is greater than I. And now I have told you before it takes place, so that when it does take place, you may believe. I will no longer talk much with you, for the ruler of this world is coming. He has no power over me; but I do as the Father has commanded me, so that the world may know that I love the Father. Rise, let us go hence."

John 14:25–31

15 | *The Castle Syndrome*

"Jesus!" I dropped the telephone on its cradle.

It wasn't the beginning of a prayer or a moment of spiritual insight, I can tell you that, and so I should have used another word for expressing my frustration. It was only 10:30 in the morning. At 9:30 there was a young man at the door who needed money for food. The telephone rang one half hour later. This man's electricity had been turned off two weeks ago and he needed fifty-three dollars to get it turned back on. His children were living with his mother-in-law until the electricity was on again, and he wanted them back. The company would only take a money order or certified check. Could I help?

I'm conflicted, that's what I am. I'm not a banker. I don't run a social service agency. This is my day off. Out in the kitchen the silver has been polished and the good china laid out because this afternoon a group of people who have agreed to help raise a half million dollars to refurbish the chapel will come here for tea. I live touching two worlds; that's my problem. I have a feel for Oriental carpets and the leaves which decorate the forest floor. I rejoice in the luxury of the family gathered about the table, in stories well told, and in tomorrow's promise. I have never been without food and no one has ever turned off the electricity, nor is either very likely. At the same time, a different world is as close as my door, the ring of the telephone, the opening of a newspaper, or the turn of a television dial.

There are many of us who experience conflict at that point where two worlds meet within us.

It's not strange, therefore, that we should be castle builders. We long for a protected space with walls high enough so that we

cannot see the poverty and wastedness which lies beyond —
castles with walls thick enough to keep out intruders, a
drawbridge which allows us to be selective in our relationships.
What we desire is a great fireplace before which we can live
peacefully with family and friends. Work is a friend, too, and
all we desire is the opportunity to do our work well, with some
sense of craftsmanship.

And so, even in a modern world, we build our castles. We
choose protected neighborhoods with decent schools. We are
careful about our credit and establish relationships with doctors
and dentists who know our names; we work in places with
carpets on the floors and secretaries who screen our calls and
visitors. We belong to clubs and are part of a circle of friends
with whom we dine and take our exercise. As much as possible,
we live in a cul-de-sac and fence our backyard.

Of course, no castle was ever impervious to attack from
without or from disease and disorder within, and that has not
changed. Modern castles offer even less protection. Marriage,
so often the heart of the security we desire, has less support
from the surrounding culture. Even the meaning of what it is to
be man or woman is in the process of being redefined. Craftsmanship and the age-old criteria for judging good work have
given way to the demands for quantity and efficiency. For many
of us, the result of our work is not easily seen or can be
evaluated only after the lapse of long periods of time.

Modern castles have too many gates, and the assaults on their
walls are more persistent. An avalanche of mail pours through
the mail slot, and from satellites in the sky come pictures in
color of life beyond the walls. In submarines and silos deep
underground, there are missiles which fly well above any protection which we can find. Surrounding us are restless peoples
who are as capable of firing guns as anyone, and the well-
trained knight on horseback who could subdue a hundred
peasants is no more. The white farmers of Zimbabwe found this
out, and the white population of South Africa will soon
discover it. Did drought destroy the wheat in Kansas and
Nebraska? Then people half a world away will starve. Did in-

terest rates increase? Then stocks will fall and fewer homes will be purchased and fewer built. Neither wall nor backyard fence will protect us from the consequences of these things.

Will Jesus save us? Will he be our castle wall? Of course not. At least it must be clear to all of us that as long as we define salvation in terms of castles, Jesus will not only leave us unsaved but also more exposed. There is no place to hide from the sights and sounds of the world around us, nor from the anxieties which trouble our sleep. That form of spirituality which takes us out of the world to be with God is just another psychedelic drug which, in order to save us, destroys the very humanity which we desire to protect. The Christian story is about the God who comes to sustain us in the world, not to make us numb with unending ecstasy.

The God about whom Jesus spoke and Christians speak is not a huckster. He's not selling anything, so we don't have to buy—even though in our churches it sometimes sounds as though if we stopped praying and paying, God would die and the whole enterprise would come to a screeching halt.

Something much more rigorous and even hard-nosed is being said. What Christians profess is that quite apart from whether we believe it, desire it, or understand it, there is a being who is other than ourselves, who willed our being, and who cares about what happens to us. We call this being "God," though any name would do as long as it is clear that this one is not ourselves. What we profess is that God is not obvious. This is not to say that God enjoys hide and seek or that he is playing a game when he remains hidden. God remains hidden and keeps his distance precisely because he has respect for the integrity which he has given us—the integrity which allows us to be gods ourselves, if we so choose; to walk away from God; to believe that we made ourselves or developed spontaneously out of nothing, if that suits our desire and the way in which we read the evidence.

Neither Jews nor Christians have interpreted this experience of God's hiddenness as indifference. In cynical moments, perhaps, or when we have felt unhelped by friends or by God, then we may have charged him with indifference. But in more thoughtful times, the hiddenness of God is central to our praise. It is the source of our dignity as human beings. Since God gives us earth as our home and doesn't stand there telling us always how to run it, we are free to entertain his help and direction. The freedom which God so graciously gives, let not men and women lacking courage throw away.

Moreover, it does make a difference to God how we live. There is behavior which is life-giving and there is behavior which is destructive. Some of our capacity to distinguish the one from the other is written in our genes, as sociobiologist Edward Wilson insists. Our survival as a part of the universe mandates certain behavior. It is what Saint Paul calls the law written on our hearts. But Christians profess that God has provided us with more than instinctually known rules for survival. He has said that it makes a difference to him what we do with and to ourselves. The message of God in Christ is that God is concerned about us. The issue for us is what we are going to do about that concern, as Abraham Heschel has written.

This means for Christians that the issue is what we are going to do about the cross, the whole event which is the crucifixion. The cross is both our way of knowing that God is concerned about what happens to us and our way of saying it. It is our way of saying that our self-destruction has been, is, and will continue to be not just our pain but a cross in the heart of the one to whom our pain makes an overwhelming difference. The issue is what we are going to do about our cruciform living, not just for our own sakes, but in response to the pathos of God, the one who suffers with us.

And that's why so many of us live conflicted lives. Whatever our genes may tell us or whatever other religions may say, we are confronted by the God known in the life and death of Christ. This will always mean that while the castle is the place for us and we are free to "castle-up" if we so choose, we will never again be unconflicted about doing so. The man whose electricity is off will always be our neighbor, whether we respond to his plea or not. The man without food will have a claim on us. Guns will always be aimed not just at enemies, but at God. Manipulative advertising, lies, cruelty, abuse of the earth, destructive marriages, maimed children, the demeaning results of racial prejudice, all of our neglect of the earth and its people, will be understood as both the shape and content of our suffering and of the suffering of God. Our doing something about the concern which God has for us means doing something about the way we live. That will mean fewer castle walls and more conflict in our lives, rather than higher walls and the absence of conflict.

Does Jesus save us? Surely not from the experience of conflict and compromise in the world where we actually live. In Christian usage, salvation means something else. It means to know hope within oneself and to behold that hope rooted directly or indirectly in the resurrection. It is the discovery that God, in the midst of his concern for us, his cruciform way of being God, is still merciful, compassionate, and forgiving. Salvation is loyalty to and trust in the reality that the love of God was not snuffed out at three in the afternoon one long ago Friday. For some of us, the resurrection is that historical event when hope was reborn in human hearts. For others, the resurrection is the way of saying that the love of God survives the experience of watching us tear ourselves and the world apart; not only that God survives it, but also that he comes in spite of it to embrace us and set us free to begin again.

Does Jesus save us? Not from the doorbell and hungry people, or from the deluge of those fleeing tyranny. Jesus does not save us from heartache within our homes, the vicissitudes of driving in Los Angeles or Boston, the trauma of being young, or the infirmities of age. God provides in Jesus an image of what human life can be in all its fullness; but to behold that fullness is both helpful in avoiding the worst disasters and a judgment on our far more common failures.

Salvation is that trust which knows that God is concerned about what we do to one another and that his compassion is not destroyed by the suffering which we invoke. Salvation is trusting that the God whose being is cruciform comes nonetheless to stand us on our feet, to take our bag of guilt, and to send us into the streets of every day furnished with his vision of what is not now, but will be.

Some of us trust him because he awakened trust within us. Others of us make a commitment, an act of will, to behave as though we trusted until that day when God works within us the miracle of faith, and what we behold from great distance is a part of what we call the self. Whether we live by faith or by longing, the conflict which we inevitably experience will no longer be a fact to be escaped, but the conflict where tomorrow is taking shape and our present life will find its meaning.